Marketing Yourself to the Top Business Schools

Marketing Yourself to the Top Business Schools

Phil Carpenter

and

Carol Carpenter

John Wiley & Sons, Inc.

New York • Chichester • Brisbane • Toronto • Singapore

To our parents
and
to our friends from
the Harvard Business School
Class of 1994

Acknowledgments

Writing this book has been an adventure for us. During the last year, we've pushed ourselves to produce a book that would be a maverick in its category, the first to take a focused, marketing-oriented approach to the business school application process. We began this book while completing our MBAs at Harvard and finished it while working full-time jobs. Without the support of our friends, colleagues, and families, this simply would not have been possible. Thank you for your patience and understanding.

Much of the richness and flavor of this book comes from primary research. We are grateful to all who contributed to this effort, whether through interviews or by passing on their application essays.

Finally, we would like to thank our agent, Mitchell Rose, our editor, Judith McCarthy, and the staff at John Wiley & Sons. Your candid advice, professionalism, and enthusiasm have been essential in taking this project from sketch pad to shelf.

Contents

Appendixes

Prologue

It was November 12—the middle of the business school application season—and that morning I found myself sitting face-to-face with John Enyart, the Director of Admissions at the time for the Wharton School of Business.

Only moments before, I had been sitting in the crowded admissions office reception area, waiting my turn for what I thought would be an interview with some lower-level admissions functionary. Enyart strode into the room, grumbled to the receptionist about having to cover for a sick co-worker, and looked down at the file he held in his hands. "Carol Carpenter," he called, his eyes sweeping the crowd of anxious faces. My stomach turned.

Enyart brought me into his cluttered office, pointed me toward a chair, and sat down across from me. He opened my file and pulled out my finely tuned, laser-printed resume. After scanning it for all of 30 seconds, he tossed the resume on his desk, turned to me, and said, "So?"

"So what?" I asked, wondering what he wanted to know.

"So tell me what makes you any different from the hordes of other applicants that come through this place. A good undergraduate university, an investment bank, a consulting firm . . . your resume looks like thousands of others I read every fall. So, what makes *you* special?"

1

The Importance of Personal Positioning

A journey of a thousand miles must begin with a single step.

LAO-TZU

The Way of Lao-tzu,1

In the fall of 1992, more than 75,000 people applied to MBA programs in the United States. This deluge of applicants meant that the odds of getting into a top business school now seemed depressingly low. That year, 4,393 prospective students applied to Northwestern's Kellogg Graduate School of Management; roughly 900 were offered a spot for the fall. Harvard Business School received 5,793 applications from more than 55 countries; only 16 percent were accepted.

When we applied to business schools in 1992, we realized that if both of us were to be admitted to the schools on our short list, we needed to come up with an innovative way to present ourselves on paper, an application strategy that would help to differentiate us from our fellow applicants. Our efforts at crafting a focused strategy for the MBA application process paid off in spades, winning us acceptances at Harvard, Wharton, UCLA, Kellogg, UNC (University of North Carolina at Chapel Hill), Duke, Tuck, MIT, Michigan, Chicago, and UVA. In *Marketing Yourself to the Top Business Schools*, we want to pass on to you the results of our experience. This book presents you with a proven, marketing-oriented plan of attack that will help you to set yourself apart from your competitors in the struggle for a spot at the school of your choice.

OUR APPROACH

If you're looking for GMAT (Graduate Management Admission Test) hints or descriptions of different MBA programs, stop reading now.

There are plenty of other books on the shelves that give that kind of advice. *Marketing Yourself to the Top Business Schools* is a guerrilla marketer's battle plan—a clear, concise description of how to develop and implement a unique personal marketing program. It's also the only book of its kind on the market. While there are plenty of publications that can tell you about the nature of Berkeley's curriculum versus that of Stanford or contrast UVA's social life with that of MIT, the amount of information those publications give you about the MBA application process itself is sparse. In our book, this is *all* we write about. We are committed to helping you devise and implement an outrageous personal marketing campaign.

OUR PHILOSOPHY

Like it or not, the MBA admissions process is a bit of a game. While grades, GMAT scores, and other quantitative measures contribute to an admissions committee's decision, the review process is highly subjective. Admissions officers will review your essays, your work experience, and your recommendations. They will develop opinions about your ability to succeed in the academic environment of their particular program, about the skills and experiences you have to offer that will enrich that environment for your peers, and, finally, about your potential to succeed as a business leader once you've left business school (B-school) behind. And they'll make some judgment calls.

So while there is not much you can do to change the fact that you got a C in Microeconomics, you can definitely influence the subjective side of the admissions equation. The crafting of your application essays, the way in which you present your work experience, and the selection of your recommenders are all elements over which you have control. This book gives you both the overall framework and the tactical information you need to exercise that control most effectively. After all, if you're going to play the game, you should play to win.

WHY SWING FOR THE FENCE?

Developing a strong set of B-school applications using our personal-positioning strategies is not for the slothful. Formulating your personal marketing plan and completing exceptional applications to support this plan takes time, patience, and a sense of humor. But if you compare the investment of time and energy it takes to produce a solid group of applications to the amount of time, effort, and money you plan to invest in a two-year MBA program, the potential return on your investment is high. If you're going to spend two years of your life and a significant sum of money to get a management education, it's worth putting in the extra effort to make sure you get a good shot at your schools of choice. And when you end up in your post-MBA dream job, you'll wonder why you ever even flinched at the thought of spending the time to do it right.

We would argue that, for those with ambition, the personal-positioning process is downright essential. The following excerpt is from a recent *Business Week* article:

> The opportunity gap between elite MBA schools and the second rank appears to be widening. This year, only 4% of the graduating classes at Northwestern University's Kellogg Graduate School of Management or Massachusetts Institute of Technology's Sloan School were without job offers by commencement. Compare that with Ohio State, where 40% of grads lacked a single offer at graduation.

The message is clear: Spend the time necessary to get into a top school. If you don't, you may end up several years from now with a degree of questionable worth.

WHERE DO YOU GO FROM HERE?

Start by giving this book a thorough reading. The strategy we outline will give you the foundation you need to develop your own personal plan of attack. (While we focus primarily on full-time MBA programs, the advice we give here would be equally appropriate for evening, accelerated, or executive MBA programs.) Next, get moving on some of the administrative items, as it may take longer than you think to get through the grunt work. While you are waiting for transcripts and other materials to arrive, begin doing your market research—it's the information you dig up during this process that will help you pitch yourself most effectively to specific programs. The hard part, of course, is writing the essays; the examples and writing tips we include here should ease the pain. As you're writing these essays, you'll also want to make sure you're managing your recommenders effectively (details in Chapter 3). Once you've completed your applications, get out and interview. The interviews are your chance to show the admissions people the face behind the words and numbers. Then sit back and wait—the hard part is over.

As you make your way through the application process, please keep us in mind. In the spirit of continuous improvement, we'd love to hear your comments so that we can improve this book for the next group of applicants. You can reach us through our publisher:

Phil and Carol Carpenter
c/o John Wiley & Sons, Inc.
605 Third Avenue
New York, NY 10158-0012
RE: *Marketing Yourself to the Top Business Schools*

Best of luck. And, in the words of a consumer-marketing powerhouse, JUST DO IT!

2

Market Research

When you steal from one author, it's plagiarism; if you steal from many, it's research.

WILSON MIZNER
Saying

Large consumer-products companies would not think about introducing a new product to a market without first doing extensive research about customers' preferences and demographic profiles. Likewise, you need to gather as much information as possible about the MBA programs that intrigue you before you develop applications targeted at a number of very different audiences. For your applications to be effective, you must understand what makes these programs unique and how strong a fit there is between your interests and abilities and each school's respective strengths. You are going to be investing a healthy amount of time, energy, and money in these applications, so it is essential that you begin by doing this initial research to ensure that your efforts are well directed. We completed 11 applications apiece and spent untold hours and roughly $3,000 in total travel costs and application fees on the application process. With two of us applying, we thought we should play the numbers to ensure we could end up going to school in the same city. Although applying to 11 schools each may have been extreme, our story demonstrates the necessity of taking the time to learn about the schools in detail before you invest substantial resources of your own in the application process.

Avoid deciding on a single school early on and wedding yourself to attending that specific program. After reading about the various schools, you may decide that, yes, Stanford is the only program where you will excel and learn. However, let's face reality for a moment. While all MBA programs are not created equal, if you attend any of the top 25 schools, you are guaranteed a solid business education. Will you be assured of the same level of prestige or the same number of offers for well-paying jobs come spring of your second year regardless of the program you select? Probably not. However, the odds are high that there are many institutions at which you would learn a lot and enjoy yourself and that would offer you excellent career opportunities. So be a pragmatist. Don't narrow your options radically before your research has begun.

Don't let preconceived notions and prejudices keep you from researching a particular school. It is likely that you won't really know what a school is like and what it has to offer until you read the literature and speak to people in the MBA community. We were skeptical of UCLA, for example, envisioning its environment as one that featured glamorous, tanned young men and women cavorting on the beach while pretending to be students. Once we invested the time to learn more about it, however, we found that UCLA's MBA program—the Andersen Graduate School of Management—is rigorous and is well respected by the California business community. Furthermore, the program is an extraordinary value: roughly $11,900 per year in tuition costs (state residents pay even less) versus $19,750 per year for Harvard.

If you had told us three years ago that we would receive MBAs from the Harvard Business School, we would have guffawed. Our impression (never having visited the school or really done any research) was one that was based on popular mythology. Harvard Business School, we imagined, was a program for preppy, Type A, sharklike individuals—definitely not for us. During our whirlwind interview tour of the U.S. business schools, we interviewed at MIT's Sloan School of Management in the morning and almost headed back to Boston's airport immediately that afternoon. We saw no point in spending time at Harvard because we thought it wasn't the right program for us. We did stop by, however, and three hours later we knew it could be a terrific fit. After attending a class, talking to students, and touring the campus, we did a 180-degree turn and found ourselves aspiring to become a part of this dynamic academic community. The next fall, we returned to Cambridge to spend two extraordinary years in a program we had almost rejected sight unseen based on stereotypes. Don't make the mistake we almost did. If you opt not to apply to a particular MBA program, make your decision based on facts, not ignorance.

FIRST STEPS

We recommend that you begin your market research efforts with these initial steps:

Review the Rankings

As a start to your information-gathering process, review *U.S. News & World Report*'s business school ratings (see Appendix A) or pick up *Business Week*'s book on top business schools. These popular rankings are produced by well-muscled publishers to influence potential applicants like you and to irritate the staff, students, and alumni of every business school that isn't ranked number one. These reports will give you an idea of how various audiences perceive the different programs. But don't hold too much stock in these rankings. They shift every year and have become highly political. The fact that Wharton is ranked first in one year and fourth in another doesn't mean the quality of the program suddenly declined. In addition, even if Wharton were to be ranked number one, if the program was not a good match for you, given your personal and professional goals, it would be senseless to apply. So while it is worth paying attention to these rankings at a basic level, do not let them dominate your decision-making process.

Request Information from Schools ASAP

Once you've had a chance to scan the rankings, write or call to request application material from, say, ten schools. We recommend doing this quickly, as schools have set schedules for applications. In addition, the various programs may take anywhere from two to six weeks to mail the material to you.

If you find yourself in desperate circumstances, you may request program and application materials to be sent via overnight mail or express carrier (at your cost, of course). After three unanswered requests for application materials from Northwestern's Kellogg Graduate School of Management, we finally resorted to Federal Express. We were surprised that that was necessary. But remember, these schools are administrative giants, and one request can easily be lost. Computers crash, mail does go astray, and anyone can make a mistake. Don't lose your sense of humor—we were amused to get material addressed to "Bill Carpenter," "Karen Wong," and "Phil Carpen" weeks after we had requested it from institutions that teach the importance of being customer-focused.

We recommend doing this market research roughly a year before you hope to enroll, if not sooner. Most schools do not publish new catalogs and application forms until the fall prior to the year in which you wish to matriculate. However, if you want a head start, many applications are available during the summer. In addition, if you are especially curious, remember that application forms do not change significantly from year to year. Ordering last year's application will give you an excellent idea of what to expect in the material that will be revised and available in late summer or early fall.

Our general strategy was to order information from any program we found even remotely interesting. (See Appendix B for the phone numbers of the top 25 programs according to *U.S. News & World Report.*) Sit down one morning before work and start making phone calls. Be patient. Many schools have only one or two lines; you may be on hold for quite a while. Getting through to a live person at Wharton was a nightmare. UVA's Darden School, in contrast, has an "800" line for interested applicants (1-800-UVA-MBA1), staffed by people who were consistently helpful and available. Beware of judging a program by the administration. We loved the people at Darden because of their extraordinary patience and loathed the "we're really swamped with calls and people . . . Can you hold, please" mentality that emanated from Kellogg. But remember, the person who placed you on hold for ten minutes and then disconnected you by mistake is not the professor who will be teaching your first-year finance class.

Ask for It All Up Front

Because calling schools can grow into an administrative nightmare and can balloon your phone bill, try to consolidate all of your informational requests into one list and ask for everything you could possibly want from that program in a single phone call. Begin by requesting the school brochure and application form. In addition, you may wish to ask for specific material for minority applicants; many schools have additional information that is not included in the standard package. Some other items that you can request include:

Copy of application on floppy diskette

- Be sure to specify Mac or PC, 3.5" or 5.25" disk.
- Another entrepreneurial source for applications on disk is a company called MBA MULTI-App, which enables you to fill out more than one application at a time. The software individually formats each finished application. The product is available only for Windows

and DOS. To check to see if your target schools participate or to obtain a free trial copy of the software, call 1-800-516-2227 or write MBA MULTI-App, PO Box 605, Washington Crossing, PA 18977.

- Apply Software Systems, Inc., also provides application software for Macintosh users for about the same price. For more information, call 1-800-932-7759.

Financial aid information

- The majority of programs claim to separate the admissions process from financial aid. However, you do want to consider this information early in the process. No matter what your financial situation, forking out over $20,000 a year in tuition will have a financial impact on you.

Schedules for interviews, city visits, and information sessions

- Try to find out early when these different events will be held. Schedules—theirs and yours—fill quickly. If you know you will be in a particular city on a specific day, let the admissions office know and make arrangements early to interview, sit in on a class, attend an information session, and/or take a tour of campus.

Catalogs for non-MBA classes

- Some schools allow business school students to cross-register for other classes within the university. If you think you might wish to sign up for a specific undergraduate or law school class, for example, you may want to request a course catalog. A few of our colleagues at Harvard Business School (HBS) had a strong interest in education and chose to cross-register for a class at the Harvard School of Education. Others took a class at the Kennedy School of Government or at MIT's Sloan School of Management. It's also interesting to note what classes the MBA program opens to other students. At Stanford, there are a few MBA classes in which undergraduates may enroll.

Specific background information on professors or departments that are of particular interest to you

- A friend of ours wanted to find a program that blended business with manufacturing issues, so he researched the available manufacturing-related classes thoroughly before applying to various schools.

Extracurricular contact names

• Were you an undergraduate hockey star? Would you like more information on the hockey team at Tuck? It's more than reasonable to ask for names of team captains or players whom you might wish to call at a later date.

Partner clubs or family activities/services

• If you are married, you'll want to learn more about the role your spouse might play in the educational community. Many schools go to great lengths to make spouses feel welcome, including them in a variety of different social and academic activities. If you have children, you might wish to request information about local childcare options and school systems.

Sample thesis topics

• Ask for sample thesis topics if completing a thesis is an integral part of the MBA program, as it is at Sloan. Review these topics and ask yourself if these are the types of issues you'd want to spend a semester researching.

This list should get you started in your research efforts. If you need additional information, you might want to turn to representatives of some of the clubs on campus—some of these organizations might have developed specific brochures for prospective students. At Harvard, for example, the Women's Student Association had developed a pamphlet with biographies of some representative women students at HBS—you just need to ask!

DIGGING DEEPER: GETTING THE REAL SCOOP

Once you've taken the first steps and have contacted the programs that interest you, here are our suggestions for further research.

Talk to Those in the Know

To get beyond a school's propaganda, dig deeper into the program's strengths and shortcomings by speaking to alumni, friends, family members, and co-workers. The real scoop will come from alumni. Talking to recent graduates can help you to get answers to specific questions and to get a general feel for what type of people attend certain schools. As always, it's dangerous to generalize, but if, for example, you meet several aggressive people from one particular school, you may wish to investigate further.

Some suggestions for general questions to alumni:

- Why did you choose the MBA program you attended?
- Did you have a strategy for getting in?
- How did the program help you to get where you are now?
- Can you describe the learning environment?
- Please describe the social environment. (Key question!)
- What did you like about your alma mater? What would you have changed?
- How would you describe the school's value set at the time you were a student there? What characteristics did students, administrators, and professors value in others?
- How strong is the alumni network?
- What value does your association with the school provide for you today?

Many of our fellow classmates also recommend finding an alumnus who knows you fairly well and asking him or her to review your application once you've completed it. If you can't do that, find someone who will give you an honest critique. We, unfortunately, did not know many alumni. Instead, Phil's mom, a former high school teacher, was editor-in-chief for some of our applications. While she did not have the advantage of knowing what business schools were looking for and what the programs offered, she is an excellent writer and knows us well. She was able to catch most of our grammatical errors (if any exist in this book, they are no fault of hers), and she was a great "BS" monitor. While we did not have much of a chance to talk to MBA alumni, we were able to track down a handful of our Stanford classmates who were in the midst of their MBAs. They were great sources of information and were able to compare an undergraduate experience that we understood to the graduate school they had chosen.

If you have a good sense of what you would like to do after you complete your MBA, seek out people in your future field of interest. Use your undergraduate alumni list to find people in those careers, or ask your friends and family if they know anyone in that particular field.

(At this point in your application process, your friends and family won't be tired of helping you yet.) Ask these people about their career paths and the degree to which the MBA may have influenced their choices and options. What critical information did they learn from business school (if they went)? What specific MBA programs do they think will prepare you well for various careers?

An acquaintance of ours had her heart set on working in film and television post-MBA. This is not a traditional field for MBAs, and, knowing this, Susie spoke to several film companies before applying to schools and asked them what value an MBA might provide to their organizations. She was told that (1) few film companies even knew what the degree was, much less how to value it, and (2) if she did feel that it was important to gain the enhanced business knowledge that the MBA would provide, then she should get the degree from a school that would be immediately recognizable by Hollywood types. As a result, Susie applied to only three schools, ones that she felt would carry some weight in the film world. Susie went to Harvard. Upon graduation, she ended up with a fantastic job in Hollywood working for a film producer, a man who respected the training she had received and the school she had attended.

Company recruiters are another excellent source of information. These human resource specialists can give you information about hiring preferences that may influence your choice of schools. Our friend Mike, for example, knew that he wanted to land in California upon graduation and, before completing his applications, asked a number of California high-tech companies where they planned to recruit the following year. Many recruiters told him that they could easily attract MBA talent from UCLA, Stanford, and Berkeley. They had no need to spend thousands of dollars flying around the country to recruit MBAs elsewhere. Based on this information, Mike decided that attending a school outside of California might limit his access to California-based companies and, therefore, chose to apply only to California MBA programs.

Eat, Schmooze, and Learn

The top schools generally hold information sessions at least once a season, if not twice, in many major U.S. cities. Harvard, for example, might hold information sessions in Dallas, Detroit, Miami, and San Francisco during the application period. These are wonderful occasions to eat good food, drink wine, ask a question or two, and maybe get some "air time" with the admissions director. (Three years ago, the consensus among our friends who were applying to MBA programs was that Sloan hosted the most sumptuous affair of the lot. To this day, we still rave about the size of the prawns and the quality of the sushi!)

The format for these sessions is pretty standard: The evening includes cocktails and hors d'oeuvres, a short speech by the director or assistant director of admissions, and mingling time with local alumni and admissions committee members. It is often difficult to discern who is in what position at these affairs. Treat everyone you meet as though that person might have some influence in the admissions process. Too often, prospective applicants rush around the room seeking the admissions director. People do notice this behavior, and it does not score points. If you are going to try to get your two cents in with the admissions director, at least be subtle about it.

Late for the Sloan session, Carol scrambled into the foyer, found her name tag, and made small talk with the guy manning the name-tag table. They hit it off and spent another 15 minutes talking about San Francisco while the director of admissions finished his short speech inside. Later, Carol discovered that the name-tag guy was the assistant director of admissions. When Carol called Sloan to set up her interview, he answered the phone and remembered her immediately. During Carol's decision-making process, the assistant director was also extremely helpful in arranging for Carol to speak with current students.

These sessions are not merely an opportunity to get your face in front of decision makers; they are also a time for you to meet alumni and to ask them questions about the program and their lives after business school. Look around the room at these gatherings. Is the group a diverse one? Do the alumni have interesting personal and professional backgrounds? Can you picture yourself in a classroom for four hours a day with people like those around you? Ask the alums what they did and did not like about the program. What other schools did they consider? It's unlikely you'll have a similar chance during the admissions process to talk to so many alumni from one school at once, so take advantage of it.

Hit the MBA Forums

The MBA Forums are good opportunities to learn more about the many different management programs from which you will have to choose.

Sponsored by the Graduate Management Admission Council, the MBA Forums are similar to business school trade shows. At these events, admissions and financial aid officers from more than 80 different MBA programs set up shop to answer your questions about their institutions. In a recent year, these events were scheduled in Atlanta, Boston, Chicago, Dallas, Los Angeles, New York, San Francisco, and Washington, D.C. The forums are also held overseas, in such locations as Paris, Frankfurt, Tokyo, and Hong Kong.

Going to a forum is a great way to collect a lot of information in a single day. Don't expect to spend much quality time with admissions directors, however, as these events are busy! In 1993, 18,495 prospective MBAs came to the events; attendance like this means the forums are hardly conducive to extended, in-depth conversations with decision makers. For a small fee (about $5.00) and a few hours of your time, though, you can pick up scads of information that will be useful in your application efforts. For more information about the MBA Forums, contact the Graduate Management Admission Council.

Visit the Real Thing

The best opportunity for due diligence is a visit to campus, as this is where you'll come to understand the true personality of a specific program. It is your chance to determine whether the school feels right to you. Your campus visit is also a great opportunity for you to ask questions of an MBA program's harshest critics: the students. Although conversations with alumni can be useful, their memories have been tempered by time. By talking with current students, you'll hear a more accurate description of the trials and tribulations inherent in life at that school. At one school, for example, we heard from many students that they were frustrated with their job searches. At another, we discovered that a key professor in their marketing department had just been lured over to a rival. This dose of realism counters the glossy brochures; it is the kind of information that is hard to get without being on campus and sniffing around for yourself.

When you are planning your visit, call the admissions office beforehand to determine what programs are available for prospective students. At MIT's Sloan School of Management, for example, "Sloan Ambassadors" (student volunteers) will take you to classes and even treat you to lunch. We encourage you to attend classes, to sit in on the admissions information session, and to interview—do as much as possible to attain a complete and realistic picture of the school. The information sessions at all the top schools often include a 30- to 60-minute presentation on the program, application advice, and time for questions and answers. At Kellogg, the information session concentrated more on the admissions process; whereas, at Wharton, the focus was more on what the program offered and the changes that were taking place within the curriculum. These sessions may be led by students or by an admissions officer. Regardless of who leads them, these meetings are nonevaluative and are designed to give you the answers to any questions you may have. Feel free to ask questions—you are there to gather information, not to score points. When we worked as admissions counselors at Harvard, we received specific questions that ranged from "How many people are on the admissions committee?" or "What percentage of students are international?" to broader questions such as "Describe a typical day for a first-year student." Ask questions about the social life. After all, you're going to be spending two years there, so you want to make sure that the school has social options that appeal to you. All questions are valid, so speak up.

NEXT STEPS

Beware of spending so much time investigating different programs that you begin to miss critical deadlines. Many of the research tasks we have mentioned may be completed in parallel. Use our suggestions as a guideline, and try to narrow your application pool to between three and ten schools, depending on which programs best fit your professional and personal needs.

When trying to determine your target set of top-tier schools, remember that you are dealing with two years of your life, two years of lost income, two years of learning. Ask yourself what will make you happy and which environment will help you grow the most, both professionally and personally? The personal-positioning process described in Chapter 5 will help you to refine this list. For now, sort through the information you've gathered thus far and make a first cut. (See Appendix C for a checklist that we found useful for tracking information as we collected it.) Having researched the market thoroughly, you're now well-prepared to begin work on the logistics of the business school application process.

3

Managing the Details

"A slow sort of country!" said the Queen. "Now, *here*, you see, it takes all the running you can do, to keep in the same place. If you want to get somewhere else, you must run at least twice as fast as that."

LEWIS CARROLL
Alice's Adventures in Wonderland

There is a great deal of administrative work to be done when applying to business school. As the number of applications to be completed grows, the administrative load can become downright ridiculous. This chapter is designed to help you get the tedious work done on time while maintaining your sanity. (See Appendix D for a chart to help you manage the details.)

STEP ONE: FIND THE TIME

Begin by setting aside a block of time during your weeknights and weekends to work on your applications. Completing multiple applications can be an onerous chore when added to the time required to perform well at work, have a reasonable social life, and perhaps maintain a relationship with a significant other or spouse. As a result, if you don't specify to yourself and to others the times when you need to work on your application materials, odds are you'll end up doing things poorly, and/or at the last minute. Consider using weeknights to complete data sheets and to perform other administrative chores, while using your dedicated weekend time to write your essays. After a difficult day at work, it's much easier to complete mindless paperwork than it is to craft an effective, thoughtful essay. In addition, writing usually requires larger blocks of uninterrupted time, which you're more likely to have on a Sunday than on your average Tuesday night.

STEP TWO: SORT THROUGH YOUR APPLICATION MATERIAL

By this point, you've reviewed the brochures included with the applications you've received as part of your market research efforts. While you probably haven't paid too much attention to the myriad other forms you were sent, now is the time to become familiar with the paperwork that you must include in your completed application.

A typical set of application materials includes:

Application for admission (be sure to sign this before submitting)
Data sheet
Transcript-request forms
Letters-of-reference request forms
Essay questions
Confirmation receipt card
Financial aid forms (optional)

If you're missing something crucial, call and ask for it right away, for, as we mentioned earlier, it can take weeks for schools to respond.

STEP THREE: REQUEST TRANSCRIPTS EARLY

One administrative task worth getting out of the way early is submitting your request forms for transcripts to your undergraduate institution and, if applicable, to other programs through which you may have taken college or graduate courses. Upon receiving your request form, the school will retrieve a copy of your transcript and send it to you in a sealed envelope, which you will then include with the rest of your application materials when you mail in your finished applications. Some schools take much longer to process this request than others, so it is worth submitting your request forms early. Whereas Stanford sent out Carol's undergraduate transcript in roughly two weeks, the U.C. Berkeley Extension Program, through which Carol had taken some evening marketing classes while working, took more than six weeks to do so. Had Carol waited to contact them until later in the application process, this could have been problematic.

STEP FOUR: REQUEST OFFICIAL GMAT, GRE, AND TOEFL SCORES

The majority of top business schools require the GMAT and, for international students, the TOEFL (Test of English as a Foreign Language). Both exams are administered by the Educational Testing Service (ETS). Some schools may accept the GRE (Graduate Record Exam) in lieu of the GMAT. You must request GMAT, GRE, and TOEFL scores (international students only) from ETS and have the official scores sent directly to the schools to which you are applying. Test scores more than five years old are generally not accepted, and test scores submitted more than two years ago are not retained by admissions offices in most circumstances. Most programs will accept GMAT scores without the analytical writing assessment, as long as the scores are not more than five years old.

STEP FIVE: SCHEDULE YOUR INTERVIEWS

With your transcript requests in the mail, your next step should be to schedule interviews with the schools in which you are interested. This is your chance to meet one-on-one with admissions representatives. Some schools, such as Northwestern's Kellogg School of Management, require interviews, although most programs offer optional interviews. Nonetheless, if you can make the time, we recommend that you arrange an interview; we'll tell you why in Chapter 9. The reason to schedule these early is that, with only a limited number of staff members available to conduct interviews, fall/winter interview schedules fill up fast at competitive business schools. Unless you act early, you may get stuck waiting until late in the application process to interview, which would delay the review of your application.

When scheduling interviews, keep in mind that you'll be better off interviewing at a particular school after you have completed the application. You don't necessarily need to have submitted it already, but writing your essays will have given you a chance to think in detail about what you have to offer that institution and vice versa. Once you know what you plan to say in the application itself, you can use your interview not only to emphasize certain points that you voice in your essays, but also to talk about additional ideas or issues that you did not have the space to address in your writings or to cover a subject that you think might be better discussed in person.

If you plan to interview with a specific MBA program, you can learn a lot about the school by doing so on campus. A campus visit allows you to interview, visit classes, and talk to students. A one-day visit can help you get a much better feeling for the school than you'll get by pouring through the plethora of business school guides on the market. You may even want to take a couple of days off from work to visit several schools in the same geographic area. But for those of you who are too busy to make a grand tour, don't lose heart. Many schools send admissions committee members to major U.S. cities to host several days of interviews. The slots available during these interview trips sell out quickly, however—all the more reason to act early. To find out more information about interview opportunities in your area, call the schools at which you'd like to interview. Some MBA programs also rely on local alumni to conduct interviews (we'll give you our opinion on this option in Chapter 9). And while it may be easier to set up an alumni interview than to secure an interview slot on campus or during a school's visit to your home city, the alumni who do conduct these interviews are often prominent, busy people, so they too have tight schedules. The lesson here: Don't wait to set up your interviews. Procrastinate and you may miss out on this key face-to-face selling opportunity.

STEP SIX: REQUEST LETTERS OF RECOMMENDATION

The next stage in the process is to arrange for two or three people to write your all-important letters of recommendation. Recommendations will provide critical support for your personal positioning, the unique space you stake for yourself in the minds of your readers (we'll cover positioning in detail in Chapter 5). These letters are taken seriously by the admissions committees, and we cannot overemphasize how important it is for you to find people who know you well to write these letters on your behalf. While a letter from the president of your company may initially seem impressive, if this person barely knows you and can only describe your contributions and qualifications in vague, uncertain language, it will do you more harm than good. Admissions staffers are looking for thoughtful, well-written letters from people with whom you have worked closely and who can vouch for your managerial, leadership, and academic abilities.

In addition, we recommend that you request letters from people who know you in different capacities; for example, you might aim for one letter from your manager at work, another from the college professor who taught your "Economics of China" seminar, and a third from the director of the homeless shelter at which you volunteer. All three of these people have seen you in action, yet each has come to know your skills and character in a unique way. If you have been out of school for quite some time, unless you have kept in touch with a former professor, it makes sense for you to seek out other references. Be creative! Admissions members are interested in obtaining as many different perspectives on your abilities and personality as they can, as this helps them to develop a richer understanding of you as a person. Your essays, interviews, and recommendations in combination yield an intricate self-portrait; it will be that much more compelling if those writing your recommendations can describe different facets of your persona.

Finally, make sure your recommenders can write well. Both the style and the content of these letters reflect on your candidacy. A friend of ours told us that he ended up with a glowing letter of recommendation that was written so poorly that it made *him* look like a dunce. Avoid making such a mistake yourself; be sure to enlist recommenders with solid writing skills.

When the two of us applied to schools, the following people wrote our recommendations:

Phil:

- An art history professor whose classes he had taken as an undergraduate
- His manager at work
- A law school professor and family friend who had known him since birth

Carol:

- An economics professor with whom she had studied as an undergraduate
- A senior consultant at her firm who had served as her manager on a past project
- A resident fellow (a dormitory-based faculty advisor) for whom she had worked as a Residential Advisor while at Stanford

While these are just examples, they do give you a taste for the diversity of sources to which you can turn for different perspectives on your professional, academic, or personal life.

You may face a dilemma when considering whether or not to ask your current manager for a letter of recommendation. What will be his reaction when you tell him you're leaving in six months? If he's upset, will he accelerate the process and ask you to leave now? In some companies, such as professional service firms, it is common—even expected—for junior employees to pursue an MBA after two or three years of work with the firm. What's more, investment banks and consulting firms will often cover their employees' tuition costs—provided they return to the company for several years upon completing their MBAs. In other organizations, however, returning to school for an MBA may be an uncommon occurrence. Indeed, people within the company may question the value of the degree. It's up to you to assess the attitude about MBAs within your firm and act accordingly. Each situation will be unique.

If possible, we strongly recommend that you ask your manager or someone else with whom you have worked in a professional setting to write a letter on your behalf. But if this puts your job at risk, you may have to be creative. Even though Carol worked for a consulting firm, she felt she would be jeopardizing her job if she talked to her direct manager about her plans. The firm was going through hard times and had had several rounds of layoffs. Carol worried that if she revealed her intentions, she'd be sent on her way within the week. To circumvent this problem, she talked instead to a former colleague with whom she had worked on a consulting project; this man had moved on to work with another firm, and Carol felt it was safe to ask him for a recommendation.

Once you have a list of people whom you plan to ask for letters, contact them to let them know of your interest in business school and ask them if they would be willing to serve as your recommenders. In some cases, this may be as easy as walking down the hall to your manager's office and talking to him or her about your plans. In others, especially if you have not spoken to the person in a while, it's best to make your request by mail. You can follow up with a phone call later; it's less awkward than calling someone with whom you have not spoken for some time and asking for a recommendation on the spot.

To make their jobs easier, we suggest that you give your recommenders a current copy of your resume, as well as a cover letter that describes why you are interested in attending an MBA program and what you hope to do with this new-found knowledge upon completion of your degree. This information will be especially useful for a professor or former business colleague whom you may not have seen recently. It also conveys a sense of focus, an attribute that business schools value highly in applicants and that your recommenders will hopefully incorporate in their letters.

The material you give your recommenders should also include a stamped envelope and the standard data sheet that MBA programs request be included with each letter. In your cover letter, make sure that your recommenders know the deadline by which their letters must be returned. Once you've given them all this information, don't simply assume that everything is taken care of. Give the people writing your letters a call after a couple of weeks to see how things are going. People get busy and, frankly, drafting a letter for you is probably not the top-priority item for those writing on your behalf. Keeping in touch helps you to ensure that everything ends up completed on schedule.

While you have the right under the Buckley Amendment to have access to your references, we recommend that you waive that right. The recommendation forms that were included in your applications will have a place for you to sign a waiver. Do it. If you've chosen your recommenders well, you should have enough confidence in them to relinquish your right to read the letters. Waiving this right shows both your recommenders and admissions officers that you have complete trust in those writing on your behalf. It's an important signal to send, as it makes your letters of recommendation that much more credible.

Finally, don't forget to send a thank you to your recommenders. Once we had been admitted to schools, we sent our recommenders a letter with the good news and a bottle of wine.

STEP SEVEN: DEVELOP A CALENDAR

At this point, you've accomplished the major administrative tasks that depend on others to ensure their completion. The rest is up to you. To help you tackle the remaining work effectively, we recommend you develop a date-driven plan of action that charts out the work you need to do and assigns target dates to significant milestones in the process. To create such a plan effectively, if you aim to complete several applications, start by understanding the degree of overlap in essay subjects among the applications for your various target schools. As you read through the various essay questions, you'll be surprised at the amount of duplication you'll find. Although schools might phrase the question in a variety of ways, all of them will ask you questions about your most substantial accomplishments or your past leadership experience, for example. Once you've seen the extent of the overlap, you'll have a better idea as to which applications you may want to write first. If you begin with the applications that have the most common questions, your life will be easier later because you will be able to lift strong essays from one application for use in another.

As you plan your calendar, keep in mind that it's best not to complete the application for your top-choice school first. If you are completing several applications, you'll see that your writing will improve with practice; so start with an application to one of your backup schools. You also need to think about which application periods you hope to target. Many MBA programs review applications in three to four waves, each with a separate application deadline. So, to complete your calendar, you need to pick which deadlines you plan to hit for which schools. Our recommendation is to lean toward the early side, although there is no need for your application to be the first one through the door.

In the case of a school such as Harvard, which has four different application periods, we recommend aiming for the second or third wave. If you submit your application as part of the first wave, you'll be evaluated in tandem with all the eager beavers. The competition might be even more intense than usual within this pool of zealous applicants. If you wait until the last minute, you'll have to contend with a greater number of applicants than if you had hit an earlier deadline. As a result, admissions committee members may end up spending less time reviewing your application. We encourage you to submit your applications in the fall rather than in January or February. You'll certainly enjoy the holiday season more if you do.

Another strategy is to apply to your top-tier choices first, and then, depending on the success of your first applications, you can later apply to your second-tier schools. If you don't need to apply to your second-tier schools, you have saved time and money.

The bottom line: Get started early. All these tasks have different deadlines, and you don't want to be bumped to the next application period because a transcript or a recommendation is one day late.

4

Tips for the GMAT

None of us really understands what's going on with all these numbers.

David Allen Stockman
(On the U.S. budget)

Taking the GMAT is a necessary evil, as virtually all MBA programs (with Harvard as the notable exception) require you to submit your scores on this standardized test as part of the application process. While we are not experts on test-taking strategies, we have drawn on our own experiences and on the stories and suggestions of friends to develop a number of GMAT tips that we want to pass your way. In addition, there are plenty of organizations that can give you the inside scoop on beating the GMAT, and we'll refer you to several in this chapter. In the meantime, here are some big-picture GMAT suggestions.

TAKE THE TEST EARLY

Many applicants end up trying to prepare for and take the GMAT at the same time that they are scrambling to complete their MBA applications. Something gets shortchanged, and, given the nature of test preparation, it's usually the GMAT. Onerous as it may be, however, studying for the test can help you raise your scores by a healthy margin. As a result, to avoid being forced to skimp on preparation time, we recommend that you take the GMAT before the application season begins.

ETS offers the test four times a year in cities throughout the United States and with less frequency overseas. (You can pick up test registration forms at most university career centers. You can also request them directly from ETS.) It's worth getting the exam out of the way early. In fact, as your test scores will be valid for roughly five years, depending on the school, we recommend taking the test during or soon after you have finished college. The GMAT in no way reflects your business acumen or experience. Rather, it's an exercise that feels very much like the SAT: Analogies, reading comprehension, geometry, and essays are the main features. The longer you've spent away from an academic environment, the harder it can be to dredge the formula for the area of a quadrilateral from the depths of your brain. In addition, once you start working, it can be difficult to find the time to devote to test preparation. No matter how busy the average college senior may believe he or she is, the level of intensity won't compare to life in the real world. In a word, get this done early. You'll be glad you're not spending hours reacquainting yourself with high school math when the application season hits.

REMEMBER—THE GMAT IS ONLY PART OF THE PICTURE

It's crucial to keep in mind that your GMAT score is simply one of the many factors that schools will take into consideration when evaluating your application. In contrast to the law school admissions process, in which you are judged primarily on your LSAT score and GPA, the business-school admissions process is a more holistic one. Admissions committee members are interested in grades and scores; but they also place a great deal of weight on work experience, extracurricular and community interests, and personality or character. Your application essays, recommendations, and interviews all contribute to an admissions committee's composite picture of you. Your GMAT score adds to this aggregate image, but it is only one element of the informational mosaic that represents your background.

That said, we should mention that different schools do place varying degrees of weight on the GMAT. And some schools, you'll notice, do end up with surprisingly high-average GMAT scores. At Stanford, for example, the average GMAT score for those students admitted in 1993 was 680 out of 800. At Kellogg, of the 798 applicants for the class of 1994 who scored 700 or greater, 27 percent were offered admission. On the other hand, of the applicants who scored between 600 and 690, 23 percent were admitted to Kellogg, and of the 36 applicants with scores below 400, six (17 percent) secured spots in the class. The point to remember here is that, in many cases, your GMAT score won't make or break you. It's simply one more data point that admissions committees take into consideration during the evaluation process.

PREPARE YOURSELF WELL

Reviewing for the GMAT is no joy, but the preparation time really can pay off. When Phil first started preparing for the test, he scored in the low 600s on the first practice test he took. His actual score on the GMAT was 670; practice gained him 50 to 60 points. The test-preparation/ education companies boast similar success stories and make commitments to their students to help them improve their scores. Kaplan Educational Center promises that, by studying with Kaplan, students will gain 80 points from the time they take their first practice test to the time they take their exam. If a student's score does not increase by that amount, he or she can continue to use the testing center free of charge until it does.

The material covered in the GMAT isn't nuclear physics; frankly, you were exposed to most of the stuff by the time you were 15. By reviewing for the test, however, you reacquaint yourself with familiar subjects, and, most importantly, you come to know the test format in detail. When you actually take the exam, you should not be wasting time reading directions for the various sections—you should know exactly what is required of you for each type of test question and be able to plunge in right away. The time you save can be well spent answering the questions themselves and reviewing your work when you have completed a section.

SPEND THE NECESSARY MONEY ON GMAT CLASSES AND MATERIALS

The classes, books, and sample materials you need to review thoroughly for the GMAT come at a cost. Test-preparation classes can run you approximately $700 to $750. If a Kaplan student improves her score by 80 points and the class costs $745, that means she's paying $9.31 per point for better results. Books like the Princeton Review's *Cracking the GMAT* or *Barron's GMAT* aren't necessarily cheap either. But if you think about these costs as a percentage of the total amount you will spend to attend a competitive business school, the figure seems much less daunting. With this perspective, bite the bullet, pay the robber barons, and invest in the appropriate classes or materials. If you can bump your score by 10 to 15 percent, then it's money well spent.

FOR ADDITIONAL HELP, GO TO THE EXPERTS

To prepare yourself for the GMAT, you should turn for advice to the companies that make their living selling test-preparation services and materials. We recommend the following sources for GMAT wisdom:

Classes

Stanley Kaplan   1-800-527-8378

Classes are helpful, but the greatest benefit you get here is access to Kaplan's extensive library of practice tests and tapes. Fees include take-home review materials.

Princeton Review   1-800-995-5585

Slightly cheaper than Kaplan, Princeton Review offers preparation classes with a pragmatic attitude and a dash of humor. Fees include take-home review materials.

Books

Cracking the GMAT, Villard Books

An irreverent book published by the people at Princeton Review. Takes amusing potshots at ETS while giving you some great test-taking strategies. Also includes sample test questions on diskette. A must-buy.

Barron's GMAT, Barron's Educational Services, Inc.

Presents some solid review material. Good for those who want to run through additional test materials beyond those that ETS has made public.

The Official Guide to the GMAT, Graduate Management Admissions Council

Contains over 700 questions from past versions of the GMAT. Good review material.

Arco GMAT, Prentice Hall

Still more practice questions. Also contains a section entitled "Test Busters," which provides some interesting test-taking tips.

Forge Ahead

If you have further questions about the GMAT, we recommend that you call ETS, the folks who actually create and administer this thrilling exercise. To reach them, give them a call in Princeton, New Jersey, at 609-771-7330.

SUMMARY

These suggestions represent our effort to make taking the GMAT a bit easier for you. Other parts of the business school admissions process can be more interesting. In writing your essays, for example, reflecting on your career path to date and attempting to articulate your future goals can be time well spent. The GMAT, however, is a bore. Focus, crush it, and move on.

5

Personal Positioning

I don't see no p'ints about that frog that's any better'n any other frog.

MARK TWAIN
The Celebrated Jumping Frog of Calaveras County (1865)

By this point, the research efforts you began in Chapter 2 will have helped you to understand how your MBA programs of choice differentiate themselves in the marketplace. With this information in hand, it's time to concentrate on developing your personal marketing plan. This chapter will help you to claim a unique position for yourself and to develop messages that will communicate that positioning effectively to admissions decision makers.

What is positioning? *Positioning* is a marketing term, a noun that refers to the unique space that a person, a company, or a product is able to secure in the mind of a target audience. Positioning cannot simply be claimed—it must be *earned*. To win this valuable, differentiated space in the mind of a target audience, you must supply evidence to support the position you state as your own. If, for example, you decide to position yourself as an expert in manufacturing, how do you support that assertion? Can you write in your essays about your experience as a plant manager for Coca-Cola? Can you describe in your interviews the manufacturing knowledge you absorbed as an operations consultant? If you can't provide this sort of evidence, find yourself a new position, for positioning without proof is mere posturing.

Positioning is not just a slogan or an image. It is not good intentions artfully stated. It is, instead, a well-supported argument that articulates just how a person, product, or company is different from its competitors.

Developing a strong positioning is a challenge, one we plan to help you meet. To begin the process of developing a solid personal positioning, we recommend that you start by spending time thinking about the product you plan to market: YOU.

BRAINSTORM

Begin with a bit of brainstorming. Grab a pad of paper and pencil, and find a quiet place to sit—introspection is difficult in the midst of the madding crowd. Ask yourself the following questions, and jot down whatever comes to mind. Be honest; no one is going to see this but you.

Professional

Work Environment/Experiences

- What aspects of your current or prior job have you found most exciting? What elements of your work have you despised?
- In which areas of your job do you excel? Where do you fall short?
- What type of work situations make you feel uncomfortable?
- Have you ever managed others? Do you consider yourself a good manager? What are your managerial strengths, and what could you do better?
- Have you ever had an outstanding mentor or role model during your work experiences? What did you learn from that person, and why do you feel he or she did such a good job?

Preferences

- Do you prefer working as part of a team or as an individual contributor?
- Are you intrigued by international business or more interested in what's going on here at home?
- Are you more interested in quantitative or qualitative work? At which are you naturally better?
- With what kind of people do you most enjoy working? What personality types turn you off? Infuriate you?

Future Interests

- What are your professional dreams? Where do you hope to be five years from now? Ten years?
- Are you more interested in product or service industries—would you rather produce a tangible good for a consumer or corporate customer

or would you prefer to develop and sell information or services to a client?

- Which functional area is of greatest interest to you? Are you a manufacturing goddess who thrives on the activity of the shop floor or a marketing maven with a burning desire to promote Fruity Pebbles to the masses?
- If you are interested in using the MBA as a way to change careers, what new field do you plan to explore? Why do you think you'd be better off there instead of where you are today?

Collegiate

- What academic areas intrigued you most as an undergraduate? How have some of these interests carried over into your career?
- To what extracurricular activities did you devote your free time during college? Did you serve a leadership or managerial role in these activities?
- What sort of academic knowledge or skills did you develop in college that you think might serve you well once more when you enter an MBA program?
- What were your biggest personal and professional college triumphs? nightmares? How did they affect you?

Personal

- If we asked a friend for three adjectives they felt best described you, what would they be and why? Go ahead and ask some friends for those three adjectives. How *did* your friends describe you?
- Of what aspects of your personality or character are you most proud?
- What are your greatest personal shortcomings?
- What character traits do you most admire in others? Which of these qualities or attitudes would you most like to adopt yourself?
- What activities outside the workplace are most important to you? Why are they valuable to you, and what do you gain or learn from them?
- Which people are or have been most important in your life and why?
- What formative experiences in your life have helped you to develop

your personal value set? How might those experiences have affected your life, and what values in particular did they help you to define?

- What effects have particular family members or friends had on your development as a person?

While all this may seem like narcissistic navel gazing, this self-assessment process is actually one of the most useful steps you will take in the development of your personal marketing plan. If you're going to sell yourself effectively, it's critical that you have spent the time to reflect on where you've come from, where you're going, and why you're interested in getting there at all.

REFINE YOUR TARGET LIST

The results of your brainstorming work will help you to further refine your list of target schools. At this point, you've reviewed the schools' strengths and weaknesses, as well as your own professional, personal, and educational goals. Which of the broader group of schools you have investigated seem to match these goals best? In which cases are your interests and priorities misaligned with those of the school? Eliminating the programs that are a poor fit means you can focus your energies on the schools that should give you the best return on your two-year investment.

If you find in your self-assessment work that you have a strong interest in international business, the Wharton school would be a great fit. If you realize that you prefer working as an individual contributor over serving as part of a team, you may want to avoid a team-intensive environment such as that at Kellogg. If you are a Southerner at heart and want to work in the South upon graduation, you might pay more attention to schools with strong regional ties, such as the University of North Carolina's Kenan-Flagler School or the University of Texas at Austin. Looking for those schools that fulfill such preferences is an important part of the personal-positioning process. Your positioning messages will be all that more attractive to schools where the fit is a good one, as the sincerity of your feelings will be clear in your application essays.

CONSIDER THE COMPETITION

Before you plunge ahead, take a minute to consider the competition. Put aside your worries; most of your fellow applicants, like you, are normal mortals who have not started their own software company at age 13, scaled Mount Kilimanjaro, or played shortstop for the Boston Red Sox before deciding to pursue an MBA. But their normalcy could be your downfall. Unless you do a bit of thinking about who these people are and how they might present themselves to the same admissions committees reading *your* essays, you run the risk of sounding like everybody else. Differentiation is essential in developing a positioning strategy and a set of application essays that will engage and intrigue a weary admissions committee member.

To get a better understanding of the nature of your competition, read through the marketing material from your target MBA programs and find demographic information on the schools' most recently admitted classes. The numbers will give you a much better understanding of the applicant pool and can help you tweak your own positioning accordingly. In the Harvard Business School's class of 1995, for example, 17 percent of the class were investment bankers in their prior lives; 19 percent were consultants. And remember—these numbers reflect people who applied to the program and were accepted! For every successful investment banking applicant, several others were turned away. For an admissions committee that receives thousands of applications a year, it is likely that the 329th consultant who applied didn't look dramatically different than the 328th—unless, of course, number 329 knew whom she was up against and made a conscientious effort to differentiate herself from the herd.

If you work in investment banking or a similar service industry, you need to realize how many other applicants will share a background similar to yours. Your marketing challenge, then, is to promote the unique aspects of your experience as effectively as possible. Did you work on any particularly unusual projects? As a consultant, did you help redesign the manufacturing process at a meat-processing plant? As a financial services professional, did you attempt to make a market for Paraguayan bonds? Realize the competition you are facing, and tell your tale in a way that sets you apart from the crowd.

For others, the demographics will work in your favor. Were you a biology major in college? Only 4 percent of the HBS class of 1995 were pure-science majors as undergraduates. Are you working in manufacturing? Manufacturing is the current rage in business schools. As American manufacturing companies struggle against foreign competition, the need to bring more management-trained talent into the manufacturing arena is becoming readily apparent. JIT (Just in Time manufacturing) and TQM (Total Quality Manufacturing) are the current buzzwords. Some MBA programs, such as the MIT Sloan School of

Management, are even crafting courses of study that combine traditional MBA fare with engineering material: Students receive both an MBA and an engineering degree in two years. As an applicant with a manufacturing background, you will be in good stead and should integrate this interest into your personal positioning program. Look at the statistics on the average age and years of work experience for the most recent entering class. Some programs continue to accept a good number of students who have only worked for two years. If you've been out longer and have a deeper, richer work experience to share, emphasize this in your application.

In summary, if you understand that you are a rare animal, you can and should leverage this novel status in sculpting your own personal positioning.

KNOW YOUR TARGET MARKET

It is also essential that you become familiar with the way MBA admissions committees are structured and function in order for you to develop an effective personal marketing campaign. The admissions committee is your target market, the decision-making unit that determines whether you'll be heading off to school next fall or working for another year. Given the degree of control these committees have over where you'll be spending the next two years of your life, it's worth taking the time to learn about the composition of the admissions committees at your schools of choice. In doing so, you'll find that these committees are a varied lot; for example, some involve students and alumni, while others do not. They also vary in size. To get the inside scoop on such issues, see Chapter 10, in which the Director of Admissions from both Stanford and UCLA describe the makeup of their schools' committees.

PICK YOUR POSITIONING

By now, you have a better understanding of just who you are, the kind of people against whom you're competing, and the nature of your target market. Given your background and interests, you know the kind of positioning you can claim and own. At this point, you need to answer two questions: How are you going to portray yourself? What major theme do you want to communicate about your interests and future direction? Your positioning will be like a musical composition featuring a primary theme and variations on that theme. You won't be repeating the same point over and over. Instead, you will support your primary theme with additional information that helps the reader to learn about other facets of your life, yet reinforces your main motif. Picking that theme can be a difficult choice, but it is one that you must make. Once you have chosen a positioning, one that you can support with evidence from your past, you'll be surprised how much easier it is to structure an application that is not just a collection of miscellaneous essays, but a powerful, cohesive argument in favor of your admission.

A good friend of ours from Harvard was a consultant with the Boston Consulting Group before going to business school. At first glance, he probably seemed like many of the other applicants that business school admissions officers see every year: a white male from a prestigious professional services firm who had attended a top-rank Ivy league school. But Rob was different; his positioning showed it. Rob positioned himself as an entrepreneur with a mind for the public good, a position he supported with compelling evidence. His essays touched on his consulting work only lightly. Rather, Rob wrote about his experience founding a thriving house-painting business, his work as an advertising sales representative for a school publication, and his contributions to the founding of Teach for America, a New York–based nonprofit organization. Chapter 8 features an essay in which he describes the intensity and the reward of his public-sector experience, an excellent example of the way in which Rob backed this positioning with proof from his past. This positioning as a public-spirited entrepreneur set Rob apart from his competitors and gained him admission to Harvard. It is a theme that continues to resonate in his life. Since graduating from Harvard, Rob has founded an organization dedicated to bringing businesses into the inner city.

If you are having significant trouble crafting a positioning, this may be the time to reevaluate your decision to apply. Your difficulty could be a signal that you may not be ready for business school yet. If you have only worked for two years and can't articulate those professional and personal characteristics that make you different from other applicants, hold off on your application. By waiting another year or two, you'll have the time to grow in ways that will eventually help you to develop a strong personal positioning. Better to wait until you are ready and able to write a convincing application than to apply from a position of weakness and be rejected from those schools that interest you most.

DEVELOP YOUR MARKETING MESSAGES

The next step is to formulate your marketing messages. These messages will be the linchpins that hold your essays together—strong, clear statements about yourself that communicate your positioning theme and enable you to stake out a distinct niche in the minds of your readers.

We break marketing messages into two separate categories: base messages and segment-specific messages. To understand the difference between the two, consider one of the powerhouse brands of the packaging world: Saran Wrap. Saran Wrap, a product of Dow Chemical, is perhaps the best known plastic wrap on the market. Dow has developed concise, effective marketing messages for this product that have generated substantial brand equity over time. Consumer loyalty is such that Saran Wrap is able to command a price premium over other branded or generic plastic wraps.

Saran Wrap's base message is "The Best Wrap for Food Protection." This is Dow's key message for the product and is targeted at the broad potential-customer base of plastic-wrap users. This message communicates Saran Wrap's positioning theme. The company reinforces this message with supplementary supporting statements, like "Unique barrier blocks moisture loss best" and "Keeps food fresher longer." Within the general population of plastic-wrap consumers, however, is a subset or segment in which Dow is particularly interested: owners of microwave ovens. Try this experiment: Take a bowl full of spaghetti sauce and put it in your microwave on "high" for three minutes. Open the door of the microwave. You now understand the need for Saran Wrap.

Dow, therefore, has developed a secondary, segment-specific message that also appears on the Saran Wrap box to appeal to the microwave owner segment: "Best Wrap for Your Microwave." (Seems fairly straightforward, doesn't it?) Again, the company backs up this claim with supporting statements such as "Resists melting, shrinking, or dissolving at high temperatures better than other wraps."

In developing your marketing messages, think like Dow Chemical. (Better that you're Saran Wrap than Charmin or SaniFlush.) Your base messages define your positioning theme and are ones you will want to convey to all of the business schools to which you apply. Your segment-specific messages, however, will be different for each school, depending on the particular focus of that program.

Your Base Messages: Setting the Groundwork

Start with the base messages. Review the scribblings from your brain-storming exercises, think about the positioning you've chosen, and then ask yourself, "If I could say only one thing to the admissions committee about myself, what would I say?" What is *the single* point about you that your target market *must* know? For Ford, an auto manufac-turer competing in a marketplace in which consumers doubted the worth of an American car, it was critical to convey an image of qual-ity—hence, the company's tag line, "Quality Is Job One." What is your primary point?

EXAMPLE

Albert received a degree in chemistry at U.C. Davis and then plunged headfirst into the culture of a biotechnology company in Raleigh-Durham, North Carolina. After a number of years, he developed a strong base of business knowledge that supplemented his technical training. This was an unusual combination of talents, and Albert decided to base his positioning on this unique set of skills. His most important support-ing message, therefore, communicated the rarity and value of his aca-demic/professional background.

Once you've chewed on the "single point" issue for a bit, expand your list of base messages. These messages should uphold your per-sonal positioning and will be the foundation on which many of your application essays are built. The clarity of thought behind those essays will be easy to see, as your writing will spring from solid supporting ideas. What other key issues should you convey about your personal, academic, and work experiences? Look for those that strengthen your positioning theme. Is community service an important part of your life? Has your training as a physics major shaped your problem-solving approach in a way that you believe will help you to succeed in an MBA program? Has your work as the project manager of a consulting team helped you learn to manage others effectively in trying situations?

Phil had several core messages that he communicated consistently through all of his applications. He had found a focus, a professional passion—technology marketing—and wrote of his interest in and com-mitment to the field. He had also found a way to bring his interest in writing into his professional life by writing for the managerial and industry press. This was extremely important to him, and he turned this interest into a message about his interests and talents that he included in all of his applications. Developing these base messages will take time and creative thought, but it's well worth the effort. These major messages will serve as the keystone for all of your applications.

Segment Specific Messages: Adding Focus

With your base messages complete, move on to the development of your segment-specific messages. As you know from the research and reading you've done on the various MBA programs that interest you, each school attempts to position *itself* in a way that will set it apart from other competitive programs in the minds of its prospects—people like you. Once you understand the angle a program takes on management education, you can develop segment- or school-specific marketing messages to augment the base material you've developed. These additional points will help you to sell yourself to a specific MBA program, indicating why you are not only a strong MBA applicant in general, but why you are a good match for that particular institution. (Note: Don't feel obliged to force-fit yourself to a specific program. If, after your research, you decide that the character of that institution conflicts with your goals, background, or personality, pass it up—there are plenty of others that may be a better match.)

CASE STUDY 1: THE WHARTON SCHOOL

The University of Pennsylvania's Wharton School of Business sells itself with two main messages. First, the school prides itself on being an international institution. The program brochure, for example, stresses the international nature of the curriculum and of the student body. Second, Wharton promotes itself as a leader in management education, a program that is not afraid to face change as it develops classes of managers capable of serving as strong business leaders in the twenty-first century.

As a Wharton applicant, your challenge is to supplement your foundation material with messages that play to the program's strengths. Consider the international angle: If you've held some sort of international position, this may be simple. But if you haven't been working in the London office of a major advertising agency or marketing Head & Shoulders for Procter & Gamble in Hong Kong, this may be a bit tricky. Be creative. Have you worked with any overseas customers or suppliers? A friend of ours who was a manufacturing manager for a feather processing plant worked in Seattle. His company, however, bought feathers from China. As he was the one responsible for negotiating the purchasing agreements with their Chinese supplier, John was able to parlay his experiences into essays that were a great fit for Wharton. Do you speak any foreign languages? This would be a "must-mention." Have you done any international travel? Perhaps you might work that in—though don't stretch it. Traveling abroad can certainly give you valuable perspectives on foreign cultures, but you don't want your essays to read like excerpts from *Travel and Leisure*. And how about the nebulous twenty-first century leadership issue? By the time the twenty-first century actually arrives, the demographic composition of the average U.S. workplace will look much different than it does today, with a significantly greater minority representation. Are you a member of an ethnic minority, or have you served as a manager in a diverse work environment? These experiences would provide excellent material from which to draw, material from which you can sculpt supplementary marketing messages that will help you align yourself as an MBA candidate with the academic focus of this unique program.

CASE STUDY 2: THE AMOS TUCK SCHOOL

Dartmouth's Amos Tuck School of Management positions itself as the general management program that cares. In discussing the school's general management emphasis, the brochure declares, "Tuck's philosophy has always been that students should avoid overspecialization at the expense of the broad, integrative talents that are the hallmarks of management leadership." But Tuck does not stop with a basic plug for the value of a general management curriculum. Other MBA programs, such as Darden and Harvard, take a similar approach to the study of business. To differentiate itself from its competition, particularly from Harvard, Tuck must define its own unique approach to a general management education. To do so, the school emphasizes its small class size and interactive, supportive learning environment. The school's marketing literature says, "While the intellectual atmosphere is rigorous, it is, at the same time, supportive and cooperative. Tuck's culture encourages students to grow with, rather than at the expense of, their peers."

Tuck also distinguishes itself from the pack by promoting lifestyle advantages. Located in Hanover, New Hampshire, Tuck offers students the opportunity to study in a stunning rural environment. Skiing, ice skating, and golf are all readily available, and the school capitalizes on such assets in selling itself to prospective students.

So what sort of school-specific messages might you direct toward the Tuck admissions committee? Have you had general management experience on which you can capitalize? Perhaps you have been working as a high-tech product manager. The cross-functional management demands of such a job would provide you with excellent material for the Tuck essays. Have you worked in manufacturing? This, too, is a functional role that often requires people to work closely with others from multiple areas, such as marketing, finance, and engineering. If you haven't worked in a general management role, think about why an education with this emphasis would be helpful for you in the long term. If you are planning for a career in consulting, for example, you might discuss how developing general management skills would help you to be a more effective project manager.

You should also consider how you can communicate your ability to function well as part of a small, interdependent group. Do you work as part of a team in your current job or are you an individual contributor? If you are not regularly involved in teams on the job, perhaps your extracurricular activities include teamwork. Does your church group serve dinner at a homeless shelter once a month? Maybe you play on a local softball team. Since Tuck emphasizes the cooperative nature of its MBA program, you should think about how your experiences illustrate your ability to thrive in such an environment and build this into your school-specific positioning.

Finally, are you interested in spending two years in a New Hampshire hamlet? If so, what about this experience appeals to you? Do you cross-country ski? Perhaps you're an avid hiker. Or maybe you're simply looking for a respite from the urban grind. If this aspect of Tuck appeals to you, let the admissions committee know why. But don't stretch this too far. If you are terrified of the prospect of living in an area where you can't get take-out Chinese food 24 hours a day, Tuck may not be the place for you. Don't try to force an enthusiasm for the environment into your positioning. In fact, you may not even want to apply. Direct your attentions to a school such as Columbia. While you'll miss the pleasures of fall in New England by living in Manhattan, you'll have access to all the extraordinary cultural resources a city like New York can offer.

These school-specific marketing messages require a thorough understanding of the way in which your target schools position themselves, as well as original thinking on your part to match your marketing message with theirs. Well-delivered, however, these messages will work—your essays will sizzle with the focused intensity admissions committees hope to see.

Chapter 8 will give you a chance to see positioning themes and messages in action. When you read applicants' essays, think about the positioning they have adopted for themselves. Ask yourself if you think they've provided adequate evidence to own this positioning. What messages do they deliver that support this positioning? How well are they delivered? What can you learn from these examples? Where can you improve upon them? The essays are your chance to put your positioning ideas to work. We hope that the examples you find in the pages to come will help you to sharpen the positioning work you've done in this chapter.

6

Diversity and Your Personal Positioning

We are, of course, a nation of differences. Those differences don't
make us weak. They're the source of our strength. . . . The
question is not when we came here . . . but why our families
came here. And what we did after we arrived.

JIMMY CARTER
Speech at Al Smith Dinner, New York City (October 21, 1976)

If you are part of a minority group, business schools will have a particular interest in you. When you take the GMAT, you'll be asked to
check optional boxes indicating your ethnicity and gender, at which
point the mating dance begins. During the application season, you will
be deluged with mailings containing information for minority applicants and invitations to events such as the Minority MBA Forums. You'll
even receive phone calls from people with such grand titles as "Coordinator of Multiethnic Admissions" who will offer to answer questions
you may have about the admissions process.

As a minority, you are part of a group that is underrepresented both
in the business world and in the graduate management academic community. As the demographics of our country shift, business schools have
come to realize that they need to train a more diverse group of managers, managers who will be comfortable with the challenges of leading in a heterogeneous workplace and who better represent the ethnic
composition of America today. Many MBA programs are making efforts to increase minority representation and to understand, in greater
detail, the concerns that minority and female applicants face.
Northwestern's Kellogg School, for example, retained Women Em-
ployed, a professional women's advocacy group, to conduct sensitiv-
ity training for its admissions officers. MIT's Sloan School of Manage-

ment founded a diversity committee to which people can express their opinions on issues that affect the lives of female and minority students.

As part of its effort to promote diversity in graduate management programs, the Kellogg Office of Admissions produces an excellent newsletter called *The Kellogg Management Quarterly*. An excerpt from a recent issue that explains some of the reasons why MBA programs are focusing on diversity:

> *Diversity* is a word we hear and read often these days. The word is used to refer to differences among people including ethnic, racial, sexual orientation and religious affiliation. We hear it often from politicians, corporate leaders, and even school administrators. But what does it all mean?
>
> Webster's defines it as "point of respect in which things differ" and as "variety of multiformity." Kellogg seeks to be a diverse community of people bound together by the goal of understanding how to manage organizations effectively. . . .
>
> By design Kellogg has become an increasingly diverse community for two reasons. First, diversity is realistic. Managers of the twenty-first century will manage in a global economy that encompasses incredible diversity. Second, diversity is right. It is a bedrock value of our society that each individual be judged on his or her merit.

MBA programs like Kellogg are actively looking for bright minority applicants to help build a more diverse student body. If your experiences as a member of a minority group have played an important role in your development, you have an opportunity to differentiate yourself by building those experiences into your personal-positioning program.

DIVERSITY FACTS

In general, most of the top schools recognize the following ethnic groups: African American, Asian American, Hispanic American, Native American Indian, and Caucasian. The focus for many admissions programs seems to be on the African American, Hispanic American, and Native American populations. Being part of one of these groups does not guarantee admission—it means that you have yet another opportunity to highlight your uniqueness.

When you take a look at the following statistics, you realize quickly why your minority status may be to your benefit:

- Women hold an estimated 5 percent of senior-management positions in the Fortune 500 companies.
- Minorities and women represent only a small portion of the population in the top MBA programs (see Appendix E).
- According to the U.S. Department of Education, Hispanics represented a mere 2 percent of the total number of MBAs awarded in the United States in the 1990–1991 school year.
- Of the almost 140,000 people who took the GMAT in the 1991–1992 testing season, just 17 percent of the people represented a minority group and only 38 percent were women. (*Graduate Management Admission Test, Admissions Office Profile of Candidates*, March, 1993).

Data like these illustrate the degree to which minorities and women are underrepresented in the world of graduate management education. Business schools are now acting more decisively to correct this imbalance. As a strong minority candidate, you will be particularly attractive to MBA programs today.

FINDING THE RIGHT FIT

As a member of a minority group, you may be looking for specific attributes in an MBA program, an environment that will be conducive to your personal and professional growth. What percentage of the student body is minority, female, or international? How well are different groups represented in the school's faculty? How diverse is the community in which the school is located? Does the school make any extra effort to help women or minorities in the recruiting process? How well does the curriculum address issues of interest to minority groups? To make sure that the program you select is one that is a good fit for you, both academically and personally, you'll want answers to these and other related questions. Appendix E will give you statistics on the representation of women and minorities at the top 25 business schools. But to get more detailed information, as mentioned in Chapter 4, the simplest route is to go directly to the source.

- When you request a school's brochure and application, also indicate to the admissions office that you are a minority and/or a woman and ask if there is any other literature available that specifically addresses the needs and interests of these groups.

- Talk to minority or women students. Most schools provide a list of students who are willing to answer applicants' questions. Call the admissions office and request names of students who have backgrounds similar to yours. When trying to learn more about Tuck and Harvard, for example, Carol called the schools and asked for specific names of women with whom she could speak.
- Talk to minority and women professors. Faculty members will often give you candid opinions on how well their school addresses diversity issues. If you have trouble tracking down minority or women professors with whom you can talk, this in itself is a telling fact.

ADDITIONAL RESOURCES

In their efforts to increase minority and female representation in graduate management programs, schools and other organizations are supporting a variety of proactive efforts. Here is a list of programs and information that you may find useful:

Destination MBA

- Sponsored by the Graduate Management Admission Council, the National Black MBA Association (NBMBAA), and the National Society of Hispanic MBAs (NSHMBA), these are free seminars designed especially for people from groups that are underrepresented in the profession of business administration. The three-hour seminars are held throughout the United States during the fall. For more information, call 1-800-446-0807.

National Conferences

- Many minority associations hold their own conferences once a year to introduce you to management careers and the MBA degree. The NBMBAA and the NSHMBA both hold a fall conference.

Campus Seminars/Visits

- Many business schools hold special campus visit or "admit" days for minorities and women. Duke, for example, hosts The Ford MBA Workshop for Minority Applicants annually to provide information on MBA programs to members of minority ethnic groups who are interested in management careers in business. This is a three-day workshop filled with meetings with students, faculty, admissions members, and alumni. Participation in the past has been limited to about 60 students. All participant expenses are paid for by Duke University.

- Student associations such as the Women's Student Association at the Harvard Business School host special "admit days" for women who have been admitted to introduce them to the program and encourage them to attend.

- The MIT Sloan School hosts an annual minority workshop and dinner with a goal of attracting more African American and Hispanic applicants.

- For more specific information on a particular school's programs, you should call the school directly in the fall to get a complete list of activities.

School Newsletters/Publications

- Some admissions staffs produce newsletters and other publications with special information for multiethnic groups. Kellogg, for example, publishes *The Kellogg Management Quarterly*. Wharton produces a brochure called *Strength in Diversity, Minority Perspectives on The Wharton School*.

Scholarships and Loans

- A number of the top programs offer financial incentives to lure you to their school. More than 40 of Wharton's 60 scholarships and fellowships are designated for minority students. The brochure from Dartmouth's Amos Tuck School states, "Tuck is committed to expanding the role of minorities in business and actively seeks to expand enrollment of students from groups that historically have been underrepresented in upper-management positions. A number of scholarships at Tuck are available to minority students who demonstrate financial need." Stanford runs a program called the Partnership for Diversity. Program applicants who make the final cut are assigned to nine-month paid internships with corporate sponsors. Upon completing the internships, the participants enroll at Stanford with a two-year full-tuition grant.

- The American Association of University Women (AAUW) awards a series of fellowships to women who are U.S. citizens or permanent residents and who have achieved distinction or show promise of distinction in their fields. For more details and an application, contact: AAUW Education Foundation, 11 Sixth Street NW, Washington, DC 20036 (202-728-7603).

- The American Business Women's Association offers a scholarship to women in graduate business management. For additional information and an application, contact: Stephen Bufton National Headquarters ABWA, 9100 Ward Parkway, PO Box 8728, Kansas City, MO 64114.

- The Business and Professional Women's Foundation and Sears-Roebuck Foundation have established the Loan Fund for Women in Graduate Business Studies. For an application and further information, contact: BPW Foundation, Massachusetts Avenue NW, Washington, DC 20036.

- The NBMBAA offers scholarships to first- or second-year minority graduate students enrolled in a business administration or management program. For more information and an application, contact: National Black MBA Association Incorporated, National Headquarters, 111 East Wacker Drive, Suite 600, Chicago, IL 60601.

STAND OUT/FIT IN STRATEGIES

If your ethnicity or gender has had an important impact on your personal and professional development, you should articulate this in your application and interviews. The challenges that you may have faced and the benefits you may have gained as a member of a minority group can lend themselves well to business school essays. If you are the child of an immigrant family, your character and outlook has probably been shaped by these factors. Write about it. If you are a woman and you have experienced sexual harassment in the workplace, this may be a worthwhile topic for the "ethical dilemma" question. If you are a Hispanic American and feel that your mores and work ethic are rooted in the Latino culture, describe how. Building your experience as a minority or woman into your personal positioning and writing or speaking about such issues will help you to differentiate yourself from others.

However, if you are a minority or a woman but do not feel that your race or gender has played an integral part in your development, don't force it. You should not fabricate experiences of discrimination or hardship in a ploy to "work the minority angle." Be honest. Your most compelling essays will be ones that address issues about which you feel passionate. Stretch too far and your writing will be empty and transparent.

While your experiences as a minority or a woman can serve as an effective differentiator, keep your target audience in mind. MBA programs are not exactly hotbeds of liberalism, and many admissions committees, while looking to increase the representation of minorities at their institutions, are still conservative in nature. We spoke to a number of our business school friends about the challenge of managing this paradox. Julia, an African American woman, warned, "You definitely should highlight your ethnicity, but don't be so different that you scare the admissions staff." George, another African American, agreed: "They want diversity, but often these programs want 'mainstream' diversity. They want to see that you are also able to fit into corporate America—a predominately white, male world." Although this view may sound cynical, we believe it is accurate. In crafting your personal positioning and the resulting essays, aim to strike a balance, to take a stance that highlights what you have learned as a result of your ethnicity and/or gender without threatening a mainstream audience.

WORDS FROM THE WISE

To provide you with a firsthand perspective on issues of import to minority or women applicants and to give you further advice on the subject, we interviewed two male and one female business school graduates of different ethnic backgrounds. We also spoke with an admissions staff member at Wharton, someone whose primary job function is to encourage diversity at the school.

Our conversations with the graduates were informal. We asked them how they had woven their experiences as a member of a minority group into their business school applications. We also asked them what advice they might give to minority and/or women applicants. Their comments follow.

Jennie Chang, Chinese-American Woman

What was your application strategy?

When I started the application process, I was sensitive about getting in on my own merits, not just because I was a minority. Many people said, "Oh, you're a woman and a minority; you'll be a shoo-in." This really bothered me. I wanted to get in because of my own achievements and accomplishments.

But, as I wrote my application and as I interviewed, that fact that I was a minority ended up being fairly important. My ethnicity has played an integral part in my development and has influenced what I want to do in the future. My application, in the end, did highlight the fact I was a minority and that I wanted to work internationally because I felt close ties to China.

When I first wrote my essay on why I was interested in an MBA and how it tied to my future professional aspirations, the professor for whom I worked as a researcher at Harvard Business School said it was boring and that it would never get me into HBS. He recommended that I put greater emphasis on my ethnicity and why it was important for me to have an international career. This wasn't a lie— I did want to work internationally. But I had not originally planned to make this such a focal point of my application.

In my interviews, people were always most interested in the work I had done in Taiwan and in my future goals that tied to my being Asian. This seemed to be the part of the interview when people perked up the most. Even though I didn't intentionally position myself this way, it ended up happening.

What advice would you give to other minority or women applicants?

My advice to people is to emphasize any international interests and especially any ties you may have to your "home" or "roots." This is what they like to hear. In other essays about difficulties you may have faced or challenges you dealt with in the workplace, highlight your experience as a minority. However, people don't want to hear the standard "I ran up against the glass ceiling story." Rather, they want to know how you dealt with the situation and how you triumphed over the circumstances.

Jonathan Ordonez, Hispanic-American Man

What was your application strategy?

My family background has had a strong influence on my life. The challenges that my parents have faced as immigrants have made a big difference in how I approach issues, how I work with other people, how I look at challenges. No challenge is too big. Imagine coming to high school in the United States unable to speak English and eventually graduating as valedictorian of your class. Think about leaving your parents behind in Mexico. Looking at my parents' experiences makes me believe there is nothing that I can't do.

As I knew that these subjects were different from what most people would probably write about, I wrote about them in my applications. I described how my parents immigrated to the United States and discussed the values that they impressed upon on me, principles that pervade my life. I wrote about my family both in essays that asked about "the most important things in my life" and those concerning "people I admire greatly"; for example, I wrote one essay about my Dad and one about my Mom for different schools and talked about their respective values and achievements.

What advice would you give to other minority or women applicants?

I would advise applicants to try to tie your diversity to an overall coherent message about who you are, so that you're not out of the mainstream. You want to communicate that, Yes, I am part of the mainstream, yet I have this one part of me that makes me truly different and brings a lot of meaning to what I do. You don't want to stand out too much.

Jeff Armstrong, African-American Man

What was your application strategy?

I initially went in thinking that I wanted to write a "color-blind" application. But when I really looked at my resume, no matter how I wanted to massage it, there was no way of getting around that fact that I was black. I then decided that I was going to be straightforward about it. I am black, and this is what you're getting.

I still cling to the belief that if you are good, people are going to want you, and if you are a good minority, people are going to want you even more. I think that you do yourself a disservice by not playing that up.

What advice would you give to other minority or women applicants?

I would advise people applying to business school to seek out individuals who are close to your thinking, people who either are at the school or have graduated recently. Ask them candid questions about the type of support that you would expect and whether or not they felt they received that.

To get further information, I don't think that you want to talk to the admissions office. Try to talk to minority faculty members. Look at the history of minorities within the school's administration. It will give you a sign about a school's commitment to diversity. Quite honestly, when I applied to business school, I did not look at the faculty in depth. If I had looked at the faculty at Harvard, I probably would never have come. But if you look at any of the top schools, you won't find a plethora of minorities. As a result, you have to make your best effort to talk to the one or two who might be there and at least get their perspectives on the institution.

Have a white male read your application. As a black man, I think that our language, the way in which we communicate ideas, is sometimes very different. I'm not saying that you should dilute any of your thoughts, but you should always have a representative of the "majority" read your essays. See how the essays flow with him; see if he understands the thoughts that you are trying to convey.

If you're from one of the black schools, I think you are in a different situation than if you graduated from an SMU or a Stanford. If you went to a historically black school, you had better be damn good. Some of these schools, like a Howard or a Morehouse, are seen in the same light as top-tier schools. But even these programs still have a stigma attached. Basically, you have to have been at the top of your class. If you were, then emphasize it.

The most important thing to keep in mind when writing these applications is to be true to yourself. You don't want what you write to come back to haunt you. Your applications should reflect who you really are. Don't play the game just so that you can get in.

You can use this opportunity, however, to educate people. I wrote in my application about the fact that I am the first in my family to have graduated from college, the first to have attended graduate school. My upbringing is what I am, and I'm not ashamed of that. Writing those essays gives you a chance to reflect on your own life. Use it. Think about the value that your culture has added to you, as opposed to detracted from you. Media and the society that we live in make it too easy to always see the negative side, particularly of a black culture, as opposed to seeing the value that it has brought to an individual.

Ms. Palmer, Wharton Admissions Officer

We used a more structured interview process with Ms. Palmer. Whereas the graduates we talked to were extremely candid, Ms. Palmer was less open about specific strategies that minority and women applicants might use in the admissions process. Nonetheless, her commitment to increasing diversity is clear, and the efforts that schools such as Wharton are making to improve the representation of women and minorities reinforce the theme that the graduates stated more directly: Minority status can be an advantage.

Why is diversity important at Wharton?

Diversity enhances the learning process; it improves what the students can learn from each other. At Wharton, we strive to enroll a diverse class. That diversity is reflected in elements such as race, gender, national origin, undergraduate major, and work experience.

What is Wharton doing to attract a more diverse population?

We have a number of efforts underway to encourage diversity. We run direct-mail programs targeting women and minority applicants. We attend various minority functions, such as the yearly conferences and career fairs held by the National Black MBA Association and the Hispanic MBA Association. We also participate in "Destination MBA," an event sponsored by the Graduate Management Admission Council that is held in conjunction with the MBA Forum. The session is run on the Saturday morning of each MBA Forum with a goal of giving minority applicants more information about the value of an MBA degree and the details of the admissions process.

Do you hold any special sessions at Wharton (admit days, information days)?

We are involved with the Whitney M. Young conference, an event that is held here on campus in January each year for minority students. The event is open to the public and is run and organized by current African -American students. We invite prospective applicants and, in the past several years, have invited and sponsored admits. This two- to three-day event has a number of panel discussions relevant to minority issues, including an "MBA in Use" session and a career fair.

What percentage of students at Wharton have financial aid? Is that percentage greater for minority students or is it about the same?

About 80 to 85 percent of the student body is on financial aid. A larger percentage of the scholarship awards that are given are minority based.

What recommendations do you make to minority or women students when choosing a school?

I encourage minority students to check out support systems that are in place for them. At Wharton, for example, the African American MBA Association is involved in both social and academic activities. It also helps with the career search by setting up meetings with corporate recruiters.

What strategies do you recommend to minorities or women when they apply?

Basically the same things that I would suggest to anyone else. I wouldn't tell them to do anything differently.

A pool such as ours is so large, with 5,000 to 6,000 applications, you really have to distinguish yourself within that pool.

Visit the colleges and campuses. Having the opportunity to really interact with the students is different than looking at a catalog. Look for the best fit for you. Also, I strongly encourage any applicant to take advantage of the interview.

Making your experiences as a woman or a minority an integral part of your personal positioning can be an effective and influential differentiator. We'll give you more information on the subject in Chapter 8, in which we present examples of how applicants have leveraged their ethnicity or gender in their application essays.

7

Writing

The only thing I was fit for was to be a writer, and this notion
rested solely on my suspicion that I would never be fit for real
work, and that writing didn't require any.

RUSSELL BAKER
Growing Up (1982), Chapter 9

With your research done and your positioning plan complete, move
on to writing your essays. This is the most painful, time-consuming
stage of the application process. If you are submitting applications to
several schools, you can ease the burden by leveraging some of your
material in more than one application. But even if you do your best to
take advantage of such economies of scale, you still face the challenge
of writing a fair number of concise, well-articulated essays. The essays
are your opportunity to convey your personal positioning to your target audience. They carry more weight than other aspects of your application, such as the interview. Well-written essays can even help you
transcend the problems of a moderate academic record or a low GMAT
score.

Given the value attributed to the application essays, we hope to give
you suggestions that will help you to write more effectively. While
neither of us claims to be the next F. Scott Fitzgerald, we each completed 11 business school applications—more than enough to develop
thoughts on how to write these essays well. For those of you interested
in more detailed coaching, the list of resources at the end of the chapter includes our favorite books on writing.

KEEP IT SIMPLE

Business school essays challenge you to be concise. When you look at
the application forms, you may wonder how you are going to say

anything of substance in half a page. Even on those rare occasions when you are given more room, the idea of condensing your entire academic and work background into a couple of crisp paragraphs may seem like sheer folly. It's not. Being forced to comply with such limitations is a valuable exercise, one that will help you to clarify your thoughts. If you are going to communicate effectively the fundamental elements of your personal positioning, you're going to have to keep things simple. When you draft your essays, strive for precision and brevity. Then push yourself further. Tighten your language.

In his book *On Writing Well*, author William Zinsser wrote:

> The secret of good writing is to strip every sentence to its cleanest components. Every word that serves no function, every long word that could be a short word, every adverb that carries the same meaning that's already in the verb, every passive construction that leaves the reader unsure of who is doing what—these are the thousand and one adulterants that weaken the strength of a sentence. And they usually occur, ironically, in proportion to education and rank.

If you follow Zinsser's advice and purge your writing of nonessentials, your essays will pack power. Admissions officers have intimidating piles of applications that they must read each season. If you can deliver a strong message in a compact package, they will bless you for it.

WRITE WITH COLOR

Just because your essays are concise does not mean that they have to be bland. In fact, your efforts to write more succinctly should be coupled with careful attention to word choice. By paying close attention to which words you use where, you will be able to craft distinct, colorful essays.

Those reading your applications will appreciate writing with verve. The English language is rich with subtlety; revel in it. When writing your essays, keep a thesaurus within reach. With this tool at hand, *manager* can become *director, supervisor, taskmaster,* or even *demagogue.* Rather than limiting yourself to the word *job,* you can write about your *avocation, undertaking,* or *metier.* Be creative. Just don't be verbose.

AVOID PRETENSION

Don't hide behind pretentious language. In an effort to impress, applicants often resort to high falutin' verbiage. Such writing is the bane of business communications; don't let it sap the strength from your essays. Good writing is creative, clear, and short on jargon. Keep *thus* and *therefore* to a minimum. Strike *it follows that* and *due to the fact* from the ledger. If you resort to the language of a lofty academic, you may have the misfortune of sounding like one.

MANAGE YOUR EGO

In writing about yourself, beware of overzealous self-promotion. Business school essays are particularly tricky. While you want to convey a sense of purpose and communicate your achievements, you don't want to seem as if you've already conquered all of life's business challenges. We encourage you to write confidently about what you have learned and accomplished thus far in your career. But where there is room for improvement, recognize this and link it to your educational goals.

EXAMPLE

While I have mastered complex analytical techniques at Montgomery Securities, I have not yet had the chance to manage people. If I were to return to Montgomery after business school, it would be as an Associate, a position in which I would manage a group of analysts. I believe that the organizational behavior curriculum at Stanford, in combination with actual managerial experience, will provide me with the base of knowledge I would need to do this job effectively.

In this case, the writer has been able both to describe a skill she has acquired and to indicate one of the reasons why an MBA would be valuable to her. Admissions officers value candor. Don't feel as if your essays can't acknowledge imperfections.

ENLIST A CRITIC

While some of the business schools make noise about keeping your essays to yourself, we frankly think this is both unrealistic and unwise.

While you clearly shouldn't have someone else writing essays for you, we don't think that there is anything wrong with getting a friend or two to read and critique your essays. Most applications require you to sign the type of statement that gives you some flexibility. The University of Chicago application, for example, asks applicants to promise, "I prepared and wrote my own essays and other written portions without professional assistance." The Wharton statements reads, "This application is my own, honest statement to the Admissions Committee." Although schools expect the essays to be your own, statements such as these do not preclude your recruiting a friendly editor.

In finding someone who will review your essays, look for someone who knows you well and is not afraid to nail you for making statements that are too bold or that simply don't reflect the real you. For each school to which you apply, you also should look for someone who knows that particular MBA program, such as a recent alum, and get that person to review your work. Alums understand the character of their alma maters and can help you to determine whether your essays are addressing the issues that are of particular interest to those schools.

EDIT MERCILESSLY

Relentless editing is the key to clean writing. When you've completed a draft of an essay, print a copy and attack it, red pen in hand. Revise, refine, and print it again. One of Phil's favorite English professors at Stanford once told him, "Never be afraid to kill your favorite child." While her maxim may sound gruesome, this professor meant that you should never wed yourself to a particular idea, word, or phrase. You may be proud of a particular alliteration you've written or a sentence you've shaped. But if, as you edit, you find the construct no longer fits, don't feel any obligation to it. If there is a better way to express the thought, hit DELETE and start again.

CASE STUDY: THE "ETHICAL DILEMMA"

As you will see in Chapter 8, one of the essay questions that is common to many business school applications concerns your experience with an ethical dilemma. It usually reads like this:

Describe an ethical dilemma you have experienced. Discuss how you managed the situation. (Harvard)

The following response to this question presents an interesting scenario. We felt, however, that the text could be reworked and have done so to show you how you can put into practice some of the principles of good writing that we have discussed into practice. We'll begin with the draft and follow with our revised version:

Original Draft

Good friends are sometimes hard to find in the workplace. At Merrill Lynch, there is one person in particular with whom I get along well. He works in my department and since we have worked on many projects together we have become close comrades.

He knew that I was working on a sensitive, and very confidential project with a Vice President in the department, and asked me about the details several times. I was instructed not to give out any information about my work, which I explained. He accepted my position, and consequently I thought the matter was a dead issue. One morning, he told me that I could find out more information about the project if I so desired by simply breaking into the Vice President's computer account. He said he read most of the material in the account, and wondered what all the fuss was about since the information did not look very confidential.

I was unsure what to do. I knew computer "robbery" was a serious issue, yet I have been socialized, as have many others my age, not to tell of a colleague's transgressions. Also, it is difficult in an entry level position to see the "big picture." I did not know the long term plan for this project, and thus was unsure just how serious this breach of security was.

I decided to ask the advice of someone more experienced who could advise me. I talked with another VP who, after my explanation of what had transpired, was aghast at the situation. He explained that some things transcend confidentiality, and that if there is a "loose cannon" in the firm who is unethically looking at confidential information, it needs to be reported and dealt with. He actually reported the incident, and my friend was not fired but seriously reprimanded by the head of the Investment Banking Division. The project was apparently much more sensitive than I could have known about.

I thought my response was both reasonable and responsible. I am not afraid to admit that I am unsure about how to proceed in a situation like this one, or in a project. It is much more important to me to do the right thing, rather than being overly concerned about looking ill-informed. After the conflict I described had been solved, I suggested to the department head that we talk about the importance of security issues during one of our Monday morning meetings so that everyone would fully understand how vital it is to our business. Often an investment banker knowingly or not holds a client's financial security in his or her hands, and a breach of trust not only can ruin the client relationship, but can cause serious damage to the company's financial stability. Our clients must feel that we are responsible and above all trustworthy people, and I learned that this consideration must sometimes transcend personal loyalties.

Revised Version

It was an awkward situation. One of my closest friends at Merrill Lynch had approached me several times to ask about the details of a sensitive project on which I was working with a Vice President in our department. I was instructed not to give out any information about the work and told him so. He had accepted my position, and, consequently, I thought the matter was a dead issue.

But later that week, my friend mentioned that, if I were interested, I could find out more information about the fine points of the deal by breaking into the Vice President's computer account. He had already read most of the material in the account, he said, and wondered why the team was making such a fuss about security.

I was not sure what to do. While I knew that information piracy was a serious issue, I had been socialized not to tell of a friend's transgressions. In addition, I did not know the long-term plan for this project and was uncertain of how serious this breach of security was.

I decided to ask a more experienced person for advice. The VP with whom I spoke was aghast at the situation. If there is a "loose cannon" in the firm, he said, this needs to be dealt with immediately. He reported the incident to senior management. Although my friend was not fired, he was seriously reprimanded by the head of the Investment Banking Division. The project was apparently much more sensitive than I could have known.

I believe my response was both reasonable and responsible. I am not afraid to admit that I am unsure about how to proceed in a difficult situation. If I seem ill-informed in particular circumstances, perhaps I am. To me, the most important issue is to do the right thing.

After the conflict I've described had been resolved, I suggested to the department head that we talk about the importance of security during one of our Monday morning meetings. An investment banker often holds a client's financial security in his or her hands. A breach of trust not only can ruin the client relationship but also can cause serious damage to the company's financial stability. If clients are going to continue to do business with us, they must feel that we are responsible and trustworthy people. And in this case, I learned that sometimes this consideration must transcend personal loyalties.

What is different about the revised version? As you'll notice, the content remains the same. There were challenging issues that we wished she had explored further, such as how she managed her relationship with her friend after the incident, but we didn't meddle with the basics. What did we try to accomplish? We began by developing a stronger lead for the essay. The purpose of the lead is to hook the reader, to pull him or her into the story. The original lead provided a less enticing lure; we tried to bring the reader directly into the action.

We also tried to tighten the narrative. Once you have grabbed the reader's interest, you need to keep him or her moving through your story. If you can streamline your language to ease this passage, do it. Part of this effort is to eliminate repetition: The last paragraph of the original draft had the clause "so that everyone would fully understand how vital it is to our business." That thought was well articulated in the next several sentences. The clause was extraneous, so we removed it.

In addition, we eliminated repetition in word choice. For example, the fourth paragraph of the original began, "I decided to ask the advice of someone more experienced who could advise me." No need to use both "advise" and "advice" in the same sentence. We rewrote it: "I decided to ask a more experienced person for advice."

We looked for and revised awkward language: In the fourth paragraph of the original, the last sentence ends with the phrase "than I could have known about." We simply removed "about." The second sentence of the last paragraph in the original ended with a dangling phrase: "or in a project." Cutting those four words made the sentence cleaner.

Where possible, we shortened sentences to give them greater punch. We also tried to alternate using short and long sentences to give the reader greater variety.

While we could have done more, we hope that we have provided you with concrete examples of the recommendations that we made. And while you should do the best you can to deliver the message effectively, admissions committees are most concerned with content. Despite its shortcomings, the original essay helped win this applicant an acceptance at Harvard. So don't despair if you're not the next Hemingway. After all, you're applying to master's programs in business administration, not journalism.

FOR ADDITIONAL HELP, GO TO THE EXPERTS

If you are interested in further coaching, we suggest that you turn to the following resources:

On Writing Well, William Zinsser, HarperPerennial

On Writing Well offers excellent advice on nonfiction writing. The book is our favorite in this category. If you buy one book on writing, make it this one.

The Elements of Style, William Strunk, Jr., and E.B. White, MacMillan Publishing Co.

A classic reference tool, this book provides tips on both usage and style. Whether you're looking for help with correct comma placement or hints on revising your work, you can turn to Strunk and White for useful, concise answers.

8

The Essays—Common Themes, Examples, and Analysis

"It was a dark and stormy night. Suddenly a scream pierced the air . . ." Good writing takes enormous concentration.

CHARLES SCHULTZ
Peanuts (1988)

Your essays are your main sales tool, your medium for communicating who you are in an honest, compelling, and consistent manner. Use the following essays as a guide, not a template. We highlight these particular essays to help you understand how successful applicants have approached several major subject areas. We hope that after you've read these well-written examples, you'll be much more likely to write the kind of focused, well-crafted essays that make admissions officers sit up and take notice.

ESSAYS ON CAREER DEVELOPMENT AND DIRECTION

Perhaps the most common question you will encounter when completing your essays will be variations on the following theme: Discuss your career development to date, your future career aspirations, and how an MBA will help you to meet those goals. In a recent review of applications from the top business schools, we saw this question in a number of different incarnations.

Briefly describe your career progression to date. Elaborate on your future career plans and your motivation for pursuing a graduate degree at Kellogg.

Why are you seeking an MBA from the University of Chicago Graduate School of Business, how have your professional experiences influenced your desire to continue your education, and what are your plans and goals after you receive your degree?

Please discuss your long-term career goals and the role the MBA will play in those plans. (Duke's Fuqua School of Business)

Admissions committees use this question to assess your direction and degree of focus. If your reasons for pursuing an MBA are nebulous, you need to do some further thinking. The readers are also interested in seeing the extent to which you've thought about and can articulate why the MBA program at *their* institution makes sense for you. Make sure that you let your readers know why, for example, U.C. Berkeley's Haas School of Business is a good match for you, given your unique set of career goals. Thus, your ability to write a strong, targeted response to this question depends not only on the time you've spent on introspective reflection, but also on the effort you've made to understand each school's program and positioning and to match your strengths and needs with theirs.

CASE STUDY 1

My long-term professional goal is an ambitious one: to develop and manage a boutique marketing-consulting practice specializing in high-technology marketing services. The past several years I have spent working in Silicon Valley have helped me to realize the need for skilled marketers in the high-tech community. The managerial ranks of many of today's software and hardware vendors are populated with programmers and engineers; this is often an excellent strategy for developing a technically superior product, but it is not necessarily the best way to generate sales. A talented marketer can be the key to driving the success of a technology company. I hope to be in the driver's seat.

Marketing pundit I am not—at least, not yet. But my experience as Marketing Manager at E-Star Systems has provided me with an excellent foundation, a running start at achieving my long-term goal. I think the Kellogg MBA will be instrumental in helping me to further develop the skills necessary to eventually become the "savvy marketing consultant"—and to make a living doing it. The Kellogg MBA program will help me to broaden my knowledge base through a unique two-year diet of case material, group projects, lectures, and more. Classes such as "Advertising Policies and Management" and "Marketing Planning and Evaluation Systems" will give me a chance to pursue my interest in marketing in a rigorous academic environment. As a complement to my marketing coursework, Kellogg's selection of information systems classes will give me an opportunity to further enhance my technical expertise. I am enthusiastic about Kellogg's commitment to encouraging teamwork. Kellogg cultivates a cooperative, team-oriented spirit from the beginning of CIM Week onward; the team-building skills I develop at Kellogg will be invaluable preparation for forming a successful marketing-consulting firm.

To be a successful consultant, it is important that I be recognized as an expert. After graduating from Kellogg, I will return to the technology industry for several years before developing my consulting practice. I also plan to continue to write articles such as those I have written for a number of marketing and sales publications and, hopefully, to publish my first book. Providing regular, innovative opinions on marketing issues through the industry press will be an excellent way to establish credibility.

When I move on to establish my consulting practice, this kind of credibility certainly won't be bad for business. Capitalizing on the leadership and team-building skills developed at Kellogg and in my work as a marketing professional, I plan to build a consulting team made up of three to five members. The ideal mix would include a group of seasoned technology marketers representing both the client and agency sides. Print advertising, pricing, direct marketing, new product introductions—we will tackle these and a variety of other marketing issues for our clients in an effort to help them make their message heard in a society and industry plagued by information overload.

I strongly believe that my best strategy for personal success in the future is to become a specialist, a marketing guru in a technical world. The Kellogg MBA will provide me with a solid foundation for a distinctive career in technology marketing. It is an essential next step in my development as a marketing professional, a step that I feel I am now ready to take after spending three years in the creative, frenetic world of Silicon Valley. The talents I cultivate at Kellogg will further hone the skills I need to be a strong leader, an exceptional manager—and even a "marketing pundit"!

So why is this essay an effective one? First, the writer conveys a strong sense of purpose; he knows where he's headed and communicates this clearly to the reader. The essay both supports and defines the writer's chosen positioning, a positioning that portrays him as a technology marketing specialist. Second, he exhibits an intimate knowledge of Kellogg's MBA program and shows the way in which the unique attributes of this particular program will complement his chosen career direction. The level of detail also makes the writing engaging—the names of individual classes can be found with a brief look through the course catalog. Using details in your writing shows a flair of precision. Finally, the writer communicates spirit and ambition, yet is not overly self-confident. Humorous, self-deprecating remarks can be particularly effective when writing application essays. Most of us don't quite know all there is to know about business just yet—if you do, then why are you applying? Poking a bit of fun at yourself is a good way to recognize this reality and to rouse over-burdened application readers.

CASE STUDY 2

I have been fortunate to have had a broad education. I studied outside of the United States at Oxford University and the London School of Economics in England. While in high school, I spent a semester abroad at Centro Harvard in San Salvador, El Salvador. El Salvador was a frightening experience, as I had arrived just prior to the outbreak of civil war. At times, I was followed to school by police with machine guns, and my friends carried pistols in their purses because family members were being gunned down in the street. My study abroad has been dangerous at times, but it has taught me the value of independence and self-reliance. I have learned how to think quickly to solve problems that could have been life threatening. Further, by the time I return to school, the majority of my professional training will have been outside of my home country. Thus, a career that involves international issues and travel is appealing.

My institutional education has focused on historical analysis rather than quantitative analysis. This has essentially involved the study of people and how their desires have translated into action. The ability to trace historical patterns or the lack thereof through macro/national experience has come to be a useful and interesting tool, one that has contributed to my multicultural character and interests.

My experience as a financial analyst at Morgan Stanley has been rewarding because it introduced me to the quantitative and financial analysis I will need to pursue my occupational goals. I felt that I needed practical experience and a challenging environment to prepare me for further education.

I became interested in international development as a career choice in particular because of travel and studies, but primarily due to a visit to Zimbabwe. I was fortunate to be the guest of a high-ranking official in Zimbabwe's government and was allowed a rare view of the political and economic climate. I worked with the Ministry of Community and Development and Women's Affairs for three weeks during my visit. It amazed me how few women were working in the development field, as well as how few women development work benefits directly. For example, child-care and medical-care issues are naturally of paramount importance to local women. While I was in Harrare, a ward full of babies died of an infant disease in the city's main hospital because of a lack of funds and the general disorder of the local relief organization. From this experience, I know that there is a need for competent, well-trained men and women of all nationalities to aid in the development of the African continent and that women can make an especially important contribution.

I feel that I can help to fill a vacuum and am ready to acquire a knowledge base that will prepare me to assume a role of responsibility in this field. My tenure working in both an efficient, well-run for-profit enterprise and in a disorganized public service organization has led me to believe that many of the management methods used in the private sector may work in the public sector as well. Thus, a keen understanding of financial analysis and overall business administration is vital.

The Harvard MBA program was recommended to me by one of my co-workers because of its flexibility. I do not want to study about the public sector exclusively. It is important for me to learn the skill of a private manager and to use those skills for the public welfare. Harvard's program is flexible enough that, in the second year, I can use the rigorous analytical training of the first to focus on some important public-sector issues. Also, after attending a fixed-income-training program at Morgan Stanley in August, which utilized the case method, I recognize the advantages of studying actual business situations and solving real problems of multinationals—or even those of development agencies!

In conclusion, the MBA program will not only teach me the skills necessary to jump over to the public sector, but will provide for personal development as well. I welcome the challenge to study in a rigorous and competitive environment similar to the one I have become used to at Morgan Stanley and look forward to meeting a diverse, interesting, and motivated student body.

This writer has had a unique, varied background and capitalizes on her diverse experiences in her writing. If you've had unusual work or personal experiences that have been instrumental in shaping your career direction, by all means, weave these into your application essays. In describing a career path as rich and complex as the one this author outlined, however, the key is to make sure that you communicate how these different professional and personal activities have helped you to develop a consistent direction. In this case, the writer crafts an essay that shows how her experiences have led her toward a career in public service. The MBA will be an opportunity for her to further develop a skill set that will allow her to succeed in her chosen field. You can use this essay to let admissions officers know how a combination of unusual experiences has shaped your career direction. But remember, guard your focus! If you don't, you'll wind up with an "everything but the kitchen sink" essay that makes you sound directionless.

ESSAYS ON YOUR ACCOMPLISHMENTS

Another "Top 10" question you will face when completing your applications will read like those that follow:

Describe your three most substantial accomplishments and explain why you view them as such. (Harvard)

Tell us about one or two accomplishments in your life that are not presented elsewhere in this application. Why are you proud of them? (Stanford)

Admissions committees want to learn more about what you've been up to in your pre-MBA life. They also want to get a better sense of what events or elements of your professional and personal lives have been most important to you. Strive for balance. If all of the accomplishments you describe are victories in the workplace, you seem a bit one-dimensional. Be bold—your competition certainly will be. Seize this opportunity to blow your own horn, to let your target audience know what you've accomplished and why these milestones mean something to you.

CASE STUDY 1

In reverse chronological order, my most substantial accomplishments are as follows:

1. In 1991, Bell West combined their sales forces to allow the account executives the opportunity to be the single point of contact for their customers. Each AE (Account Executive) was reassigned to new accounts with a greatly expanded product line from which to sell. My responsibility was to provide sales support for all voice and data equipment that Bell West sold as a third-party distributor. However, these product lines were new to most of the reorganized sales force and included approximately 60 different products. Without training, the sales force was operating in a void. I developed a plan and implemented a package that made the necessary information and sales tools readily accessible to the sales force.

The package included the following parts: I collected all the information possible on each product and compiled a set of 27 reference guides to be placed in a handbook with pictures and overview information of each product in the product line, small enough to accompany the sales person on customer visits. To make ordering product brochures and sales collateral easier, I managed the loading of all collateral (approximately 1,000 pieces) into a centralized database that could be accessed from each sales office through the touch tone telephone pad. The orders were then routed automatically to the appropriate manufacturer, who filled the order. To speed the communication flow, I developed a contact list of product-support personnel. I established three methods of distributing new-product information. If extremely timely delivery was required, voice mail or the group fax network was used. Otherwise, information was sent via company mail to the sales managers.

I implemented all of these changes within eight months of the reorganization. I worked with many other staff organizations within Bell West to implement these programs and to evaluate their effectiveness. The responses I received from sales have been extremely positive. Sales of equipment lagged in the first half of 1991, but in the latter half, sales increased. I successfully developed a package that provides easy access to information the AEs need to sell, thereby increasing revenues for Bell West.

2. In an effort to visually depict the effects of time upon memory, a theme that pervades all my artwork, I embarked upon an ambitious art project in printmaking. As I was a novice to printmaking, my professor was stunned by the massive scope and complexity of the project I proposed. From start to finish, the project took over 120 hours to complete and required many intermediate steps. The final outcome is a large representation of a wrinkled and stained block quilt that has been shown in three different exhibits in Charlottesville, Virginia, and Alexandria, Virginia. It has become the cornerstone of my existing portfolio.

The "quilt" is comprised of 97 separate metal plates, some as small as 1 inch by 1 inch. A separate image is etched onto each plate using acid. Once the plates were completed, each was inked and wiped by hand and arranged properly on the press. Then, paper was pressed into the plates, lifting the ink to create the image. The inking process must be done for every print, and it alone requires eight to ten hours of continuous work. It took many attempts before I could obtain a tone-consistent print. The print was painted, stained, collaged, and sewn to create the finished product. This project required tremendous development of skill in a short period of time. It also demonstrated my perseverance and patience. Lastly, it categorized me as a risk-taker, for with every new step, the potential for ruining the final piece became more likely.

3. In 1989, I acted as the Account Executive for the UVA (University of Virginia) chapter of the American Advertising Federation. I managed the group's development of a complete marketing and advertising campaign for a new product introduction by the Kellogg Company. I led the club in every aspect of campaign development, including performing and analyzing research to select a target audience, product name, positioning, pricing, and packaging, and managed a corresponding budget of $40,000. I orchestrated the creation of innovative marketing, media and pro-

motional strategies, including the scheduling and creative executions. I kept the project on course and the people focused on the objectives set at the beginning of the campaign development. The campaign was completed in two and a half months. I compiled and published the campaign plans book, which included the club's research and proposals. Finally, I presented the UVA campaign at the American Advertising Federation competition in North Carolina. In addition to managing this massive project and the people involved, I took six classes that semester and maintained a grade point average of 3.9.

In this essay, the writer exhibits both the breadth and depth of her accomplishments in describing a number of enterprising projects she has undertaken. The writer uses the essay to provide solid support for her positioning, which casts her as a strong manager with a creative flair. Rather than confine her writing to events in the workplace, she describes laudable achievements in several areas—work, extracurricular activities, and school—which shows she is no mere one-legged applicant. The writing is precise and rich with descriptive detail that helps the reader to develop a true understanding and appreciation of what she has done. Just as the "quilt" the author described is composed of a multiplicity of tiny metal plates, so are your essays a mosaic of hundreds of well-chosen words. The more critical detail you include, the better you "word-smith" your writing, the more vibrant the picture you create for the reader.

The essay also reflects this writer's understanding of some of the personal qualities for which MBA programs look in evaluating candidates: perseverance, attention to detail, the ability to manage a project successfully, and the willingness to take risks. If these are aspects of your personality, too, make them clear in your writing. The applicant's perseverance is apparent in all three activities she describes. She is clearly comfortable managing complex projects and is attentive to detail; the description of the painstaking work required to create the "quilt" is a case in point. By specifying the size of her marketing and advertising budget, the applicant allows the reader to get a good feel for the magnitude of her work. Finally, the writer conveys her willingness to take risks. Making calculated risks is essential for success in business, an issue that the readers of your applications know well. The writer's readiness to confront and manage risk in both her professional and extracurricular activities is a characteristic that admissions staffers will find attractive.

CASE STUDY 2

During my senior year in college I was elected President of the Student Association (SA). My election victory was an upset of the traditional "government group," most of whom had targeted this most coveted position during their freshman year and had proceeded to run for numerous class and SA offices to gain the necessary exposure. I, on the other hand, founded a much-needed Black Student Association (BSA) to help pump some life into the apathetic student environment at Trinity. I decided not to get caught in the slow-moving wheels of the SA bureaucracy but, instead, extended my energies where I thought they would be of the most value. I was elected on the basis of my service to the college community.

The election was a nasty one, as I was running against the Vice President of the Student Association. I was accused of being biased because of my role in founding the BSA and of being unqualified to be the leader of the student population. However, many voters thought that if I could help to revitalize a group that lacked funds, a system for operation, and whose members were discouraged because of their lack of confidence, and help change that group into the most active group on campus, then I could run a student government.

My victory was the start of a revolution at Trinity. The makeup of student government has since changed markedly. The influx of new people and ideas has benefited the college on the whole, and participation in college activities is now more reflective of the diverse student environment. My administration was for the community, and we had an overwhelming response. During that year, three new clubs asked for charters, and the Commuter Students Club got more involved in life on campus because we gave them an office where they could organize activities. Even the International Students Union became more active by holding a successful lecture series for which ambassadors from the many countries represented by club members were invited to speak on topics relating to their past or present national experience.

I was pleased that I was able to accomplish my goal for promoting more activity at Trinity. I never backed down during the election nor during my tenure in office, even when political situations seemed impossible. I learned to become a political tactician in order to accomplish what I thought was best for our school. Most of all, I was pleased that my multicultural experience has provided me with the ability to transcend racial barriers. I learned to handle a responsible leadership position in a predominantly white environment where the racial climate was sometimes volatile and received the respect of not only my black peers, but my white ones as well.

At the close of the 1984-85 academic year, I was chosen by *Glamour* magazine as one of the "Top Ten College Women of 1984-85." This distinction was based upon academic achievement, recommendations by the president of the college and the Dean of Students, and a written essay entitled "My Most Significant College Experiences." I wrote openly and honestly about my desire to understand my place as a black woman in America's "melting pot" and the difficulties involved in assuming a leadership position in a segregated college community. I found out later that my leadership abilities and my compelling essay set me apart from the 3,000 other women who applied for the competition in 1985.

I won a trip to New York City for one week to see the sights and to meet with the nine other women who had received this distinction. It was a remarkable experience to be with nine other people who had this same high energy level! Needless to say, we did not get much sleep that week as we spent our time talking about our views, hopes, and dreams. I was also entitled to a cash award and the chance to meet with one person of my choice. I chose to meet with an African ambassador to the United Nations who, during our lunch, explained his country's plans for development and the numerous problems involved in trying to educate his people in a Western context. I maintain contact with him and hope that once I obtain the necessary skills, I can give my support to his innovative projects.

The last and most exciting part of this experience was the chance to appear in the August 1985 issue of the magazine. It was great fun being famous for a month!

In August 1987, I married Jordan Thomas Jackson in New York, and this is by far my greatest accomplishment. I am proud of him. It finally hit me after the "pomp and circumstance" of the wedding that I had said vows that would bind me to one person for the rest of my life. The decision to marry is the single most important one I will ever make and will provide me with the greatest of life's rewards.

This essay conveys a strong sense of balance. The author writes about three very different events with enthusiasm and pride. While we do not mean to suggest that it is mandatory to portray yourself as some sort of DaVinci-esque "ultimate renaissance person," we do recommend that you use the essay to show your accomplishments in a number of different areas. It is also important to realize that one need not claim one's greatest accomplishment to be a professional one. For this writer, it is her marriage—not the deal she brokered with a major chemical company or the bonds she sold for a highway construction project—that she feels is her greatest triumph. If yours, too, is personal victory, by all means write about it! A tremendous personal accomplishment carries no less weight in the minds of admissions committee members than does a professional one. Moreover, if it means that much to you, you will end up writing about that occurrence much more effectively than if you are describing some professional event or transaction that you think will impress an admissions committee. Finally, note the way in which the writer cross-references a theme developed in an earlier essay. Here, too, she notes her interest in African development work. Where you have the opportunity to make this sort of reference, do so, as it further reinforces your positioning points in the minds of the readers.

ESSAYS ON DISTINCTIVENESS/CONTRIBUTION

Admissions committees want to know what makes you different from the thousands of other applicants they encounter each fall. An increasing number of them are beginning to ask for this information outright:

> *The Darden School seeks a diverse and unique entering class of future managers. How will your distinctiveness enrich our learning environment and enhance your prospects for success as a manager?(University of Virginia)*

In a diverse learning community, students come to the table with a wide assortment of different skills and experiences that they share with one another, both in the classroom and outside it. All MBA programs aspire to create this sort of learning environment, and they want to know what particular elements of your persona will contribute to the interactive, educational chemistry of their institution.

CASE STUDY

I believe I am distinctive in many respects. Superficially, I look different from the majority of the American population. Realistically, I am different from the majority of the American population. Growing up in the rural town of Fairmont, West Virginia, I was acutely aware of the fact that I am Chinese. I had to work very hard to make people look beyond superficialities like a Chinese name (Wu). Realizing that my external appearance would be subconsciously held against me by others in Fairmont, I concentrated on developing my subcutaneous qualities such as intellect, attitude, and personality.

Like the majority of Chinese parents, mine instilled a strong work ethic in their children. Given our unique geographical circumstances, they modified their lecture to include "because of your appearance, you must work even harder than your peers to be recognized." As a result, I am dedicated, ambitious, industrious, and accepting of challenges. I do not believe in leaving a task undone; at Salomon Brothers Inc, I often worked 100-hour weeks to complete a project. At Deloitte & Touche, I have also worked long hours to meet deadlines for deliverables. My strong work ethic and positive attitude carried me onto many projects where I further developed my technical skills. Currently, I am responsible for the high-level design and implementation of an expert system. Through classes, experience, and my own initiative, I have learned to use tools and languages such as Nexpert Object, SQL*FORMS, and UNIX. In addition, my parents stressed a high standard of quality in whatever I pursued. This meant being a student-body officer and toiling through all the trivialities to put on the best prom ever in high school. In college, I reworked a lecture three times for the Technical Communications class I taught in the Engineering department. At Salomon, I exhibited perverse attention to detail while experiencing insane "all-nighters" and other physical and mental marathons. Currently, as a management consultant in information technology, I continuously review deliverables and learn technical details during personal time. These traits of mine—dedication, the willingness to work hard, a commitment to quality—are part of the potential contribution I can make to Darden and to any future employer.

Personal qualities, such as industriousness, have certainly

brought me recognition. However, the ability to motivate my peers is also important to me. While the job functions I performed at Salomon Brothers Inc and Deloitte & Touche are different, I believe that the same qualities have made me successful in both positions. I have a positive attitude, and, while I can be intense, I am not insipid. My attitude encompasses a "can-do" thought process (inculcated at Stanford and further entrenched at Salomon). I believe that, if I want to accomplish a task, I can and will. The combination of intelligence with a positive attitude leads to results. My optimism helps to encourage and motivate the people with whom I work. At Darden and in a managerial setting, my "can-do" attitude will support and mobilize team members.

Another distinctive quality is my ability to interact with people with different backgrounds. I am comfortable in a variety of environments and manage to feel at ease with almost anyone. This attribute has enhanced my personal and professional growth throughout my life. I managed to initiate conversation and endure, without a hint of laughter, a recognition luncheon with the Daughters of the American Revolution as the outstanding high school student of the year. At Salomon, I was thrown into many boardrooms and printing sessions with CEOs, CFOs, lawyers, and other key members of management. And, at Deloitte, through meeting facilitation and presentations, I have strengthened my oral and verbal communication skills. My strong interpersonal skills enable me to work well in teams, an asset that will complement the Darden environment and also help me to become a better manager.

The challenges of my hometown environment and my work experiences have sharpened two additional tools over the years. A sense of humor and flexibility have enabled me to cope with any challenge. In grade school, I utilized my sense of humor to deal with the pain of being "different." At Salomon, the ability to laugh at myself helped me to cope with stressful working conditions, and my flexibility enabled me to work quickly and make decisions in a rapidly changing environment. At Deloitte, I often use humor to defuse tense meetings and to help my co-workers relax. In the fast-paced, challenging classrooms and study groups of Darden, laughter can be an excellent tool for defusing tension and for building camaraderie.

I am thankful that I grew up in a community in which my appearance was distinctive. The situation forced me to develop a personality and an intellect for which I am remembered. With a deeply instilled work ethic, strong interpersonal skills, a high level of motivation, and excellence, I believe I will enrich the educational and social environment at Darden and continue to grow as a manager.

In drafting your business school essays, remember this simple bit of wisdom: "Answer the question that is asked." This may seem obvious; in reality, however, applicants often are tempted to shoehorn information that they want to relay into responses that simply don't answer the questions the admissions committee has posed. This author nails the question at hand with a precise, detailed essay, constructing a solid argument built on specific examples—a technique you can use in essays of your own. She conveys a positive attitude and a strong work ethic, which are essential in any rigorous MBA program. She also ties her strengths to opportunities at Darden. Finally, she deals with her minority status convincingly. Her identity as both a woman and a minority was a cornerstone of this woman's personal positioning. As we discuss in Chapter 6, if you are a member of a minority group, we recommend you emphasize this important competitive advantage in your writing. Although business schools are still overwhelmingly populated with white males, many are making extraordinary efforts to increase the gender and racial diversity of their student body. As an ethnic minority, as a woman, or as a representative of both camps, you are a valuable property to MBA programs.

ESSAYS ON INTERNATIONAL EXPERIENCES

Over the past several years, business school curriculums have become increasingly international in nature, a recognition of the fact that barriers such as regional boundaries, cultural differences, and geographic distances that have hampered international business in the past are breaking down. As business becomes more global in nature, the next generation of business leaders in this country and the world will need a more international perspective to be successful managers. MBA programs are attempting to adjust to this new reality. In addition to changing their own course offerings, they are also looking for a greater degree of international experience when evaluating applicants. Questions such as these are appearing on MBA applications with increasing frequency:

Describe any significant study, employment, or travel outside your home country. Why did you pursue your experience abroad, how long did you stay (include dates), and did it enhance your foreign language skills? (University of Chicago)

Discuss the effect that an increasingly global economy may have on your future responsibilities as a manager, both generally and as regards your chosen field, and what you hope to learn at MIT to enable you to meet this challenge. (MIT's Sloan School of Management)

There are many social, political, and economic challenges facing the world today. Which issue is the most important to you, and why? (University of Pennsylvania's Wharton School of Management)

CASE STUDY 1

As the global economy has become more tightly integrated, it has become harder for American firms to ignore the world beyond the Yankee border. Not only are overseas markets a place for sales, they are a vital source of financing, technical innovation, skilled labor, and more. For example, the computing industry has been transformed by the integrated global economy. Over 85 percent of the networking products that I developed at Hewlett-Packard are sold in Asia and Europe. Many Silicon Valley and Route 128 startups today get their venture capital funds from Japan. All of these changes have forced managers to become more international.

The globalization of the economy has already touched my career. At Hewlett-Packard, I was the lead engineer for the development of the world's first UNIX-based Asian IBM terminal emulator. The organization of this project was that of a chimera that acted like a hydra with nine fiercely independent heads. Engineering was done by American, Japanese, and Taiwanese engineers in the United States. Marketing came from Singapore, while testing took place in Korea, Taiwan, and Japan. The project manager was a Taiwanese expatriate based in the United States.

Funding came from Asian and American divisions, and sales were to be worldwide. It was hard to get this beast to agree quickly on product definition, development, and sales questions because so many different needs, viewpoints, languages, and cultures were involved.

That is the challenge of the global manager. The global manager must be adept at bridging cultures, must be fluent in foreign tongues and practices, and must be skilled at recognizing opportunities and threats in markets across the world. Having lived in Australia for two years, traveled the world extensively, worked on an international software development project, and studied Japanese and French for several years, I believe that I can cross cultures well.

But there is much more for me to learn about recognizing and responding to international opportunities and threats. For example, in the software industry, the emergence of the Japanese "software factory" holds the promise of faster, higher-quality software development. The transfer of software-development work from engineers based in the United States and Europe to equally well-educated engineers in India offers the opportunity to reduce the high cost of software development. But each of these international changes is a threat to American software firms that compete in an open global economy. American managers will catch the wave of these innovations, or they will be drowned by them.

MIT can teach me to ride the wave. At the suggestion of one of my recommenders, Professor Michael Meyerowitz, I met with MIT Professor Jeff Burchill last spring and talked with him about his research into the Japanese software industry. I am sure I could learn much from him about the nation that is at once America's greatest partner and competitor. I expect that the Leaders For Manufacturing (LFM) Pro-Seminars will also give me the opportunity to quiz professionals from many industries about how they identify and exploit foreign opportunities and how they recognize and react to foreign threats. My LFM master's thesis might focus on comparative international approaches to high-quality software manufacturing.

A global economy requires global managers. As the American slice of the world's economic pie continues to shrink and as its technological advantage over its international competitors grows ever smaller, the success of American firms will depend on the ability of their managers to build, sell, and service products that are better, faster, and cheaper than those of their competitors. This success will require those managers to work with foreign suppliers and customers, to follow foreign markets, and to attack foreign competitors. This is difficult to do, but an open world economy leaves us with no choice. MIT will teach me how to be a global manager by giving me basic skills in accounting, economics, decision making, etc., by outfitting me with the confidence and tools to deal with change and by helping me to understand how to integrate engineering and management in the manufacture of excellent products. When combined with international understanding and experience, this should make me a good global manager.

The writer clearly identifies many of the reasons why it is essential for today's managers to develop a global business perspective. He also shows that he already has a good head start. If you can impart your application with an international flavor, do so. The challenges of global management are gaining increased attention in business schools, and, as this essay shows, this writer can leverage his extensive international experiences to support a positioning that includes a strong international component.

For some of you, the international questions may be more of a stretch, but be creative with what you've got. If you have foreign language skills or international business experience, leverage these assets; they will serve you well in your efforts to differentiate yourself from the crowd. This author has both of those assets and puts them to good use; he communicates his experience well, and highlights his enthusiasm for the opportunities in his field of expertise that will come with the globalization movement. The writer also links his interests with precise opportunities available at MIT, indicating the degree of effort he has made to explore the school's offerings in depth. Finally, he overtly recognizes the academic areas in which he needs additional training, thus reemphasizing the degree to which the Sloan master's program will serve as an important part of his professional development. We recommend you do the same where possible. Rather than admitting a weakness, you are instead illustrating personal and professional maturity—you know your weak spots, and you are interested in using the MBA at "School X" as an opportunity to strengthen your knowledge in those particular areas.

CASE STUDY 2

"The only thing comparable to what's going on in China is the reconstruction of postwar Europe under the Marshall Plan," says Rajendra Nath, Beijing general manager for GE Aircraft Engines in the May 17, 1993, issue of *Business Week*. Nath refers to the economic growth of the country (China). To me, the economic development of China represents the most important challenge facing the world today; its success would drive the global economy with its manufacturing, size, need for capital, and market potential.

If China develops, it would provide an unmatched manufacturing source for the world's producers. Based on manufacturing, Guandong Province in southern China has demonstrated success in this area and has produced one of the fastest growing economic areas in the world. This growth demonstrates that the country can manufacture successfully. If costs in the coastal regions rise, these same skills could be transferred to inland provinces to maintain competitive rates. This proven manufacturing capability and the huge supply of inexpensive labor ensure that China's role in global manufacturing would only grow.

China's economic size would increasingly drive the world's economy. Many economists predict that China's gross domestic product will grow enough in the next decade to make it "one of the world's top five economic powers," according to *Business Week*. Today the economies of the United States, Japan, and Germany shape the state of the world's economies because of their large sizes. Likewise, tomorrow, China's economy would lead the global economy with its strong growth rates.

The economic development of China also would lead to a tremendous need for foreign capital. For example, development requires infrastructure in transportation, energy, and communications that China presently lacks. The country needs capital to fund the building of this infrastructure. Recently, a Hong Kong businessman funded a $1.2 billion highway in southern China to fill a transportation need. This demonstrates how China requires foreign capital to invest in necessary basic foundations for which the country cannot provide funds on its own. The need for foreign capital to invest in China would attract funds from the global economy and would only grow as the country's economy develops.

The enormous market potential of China would also power the world's economy. With 1.2 billion people, China represents the largest single market in the world. Telecommunications and aerospace companies already recognize the potential of the country. For instance, Boeing expects that "China will buy $40 billion in commercial jets from the United States and Western Europe over the next 20 years. That means China will rank second only to Japan (in commercial jet purchases)," states *Business Week*. This market potential would shape the global economy as companies tap into it.

The world should see the economic challenge facing China as the most important one today because its success would propel the global economy into tomorrow. This significance explains in part why I want to help China face this challenge. The MBA offers me the business education that will prepare me to contribute to the development of the Chinese economy; however, the Wharton/Lauder program goes beyond other MBAs by enabling me to also face the internal aspect of this challenge.

This essay is a response to the question posed by the Wharton School. It was written by a friend of ours who had just returned from a two-year stint teaching English in northern China. This essay clearly describes the extraordinary growth of the Chinese economy and some of the corresponding business opportunities. If the growth continues at such a rate, China will indeed have a significant effect on the global economic structure, and, as the writer indicates, both countries and companies must take note and plan accordingly.

In this essay itself, the author says less about why this expansion is important to him than you would think might be appropriate. When viewed in the context of the rest of his application, however, this is not a problem. In several of his other essays, the candidate describes his experiences in China and his interest in developing a career in which he will do business that will take him back to China to help in its growth and to profit from it. As a result, in both this essay and in the rest of his application, the writer has positioned himself as someone with a specific international focus, someone who would benefit greatly from a business school program with a strong international flair. Given the international nature of the Wharton School, this is a perfect positioning strategy for applying to that program. Wharton's admissions officers agreed and admitted him to the Class of 1996.

ESSAYS ON ETHICAL DILEMMAS

While we don't believe that any business school can claim to *teach* ethics, many offer courses that expose students to ethically controversial situations to prompt students to think about what they might do as managers in similar circumstances. Harvard, for example, offers electives such as "Moral Dilemmas of Management." Business ethics is a cornerstone of the educational philosophy of the University of Virginia (UVA). All first-year students at UVA's Darden School enroll in a required ethics module. Given this emphasis in today's MBA curriculums, it makes sense that the subject of ethics would rear its head during the application process. Typical questions include:

> *Describe an ethical dilemma that you have personally encountered. What alternative actions did you consider and why? Do **not** tell us what you decided to do. (For purposes of this question, ethical is defined as "in accordance with accepted principles of conduct.") (Stanford)*

> *What is the most difficult ethical dilemma you have faced in your professional life? Articulate the nature of the difficulty. Upon present reflection, would you have resolved this dilemma in a different manner? (UVA)*

For many of you, writing a response to the "ethical dilemma" questions will begin with wracking your brains to come up with something to write about in the first place! You may not have encountered a situation that was all that ethically questionable during the couple of years you've spent in the working world. Or, even if you have an idea, it may not seem to be overly intriguing. "How am I going to make this issue sound sexy?" you wonder. But as you think back on your career, issues that you shrugged off in the past may now present editorial opportunities as you reflect upon them with the benefit of hindsight. Be creative. For other people, however, this question will give you a chance to tell a tale you've been itching to reveal for quite some time. If this is the case, go to it! But remember, the purpose of this question is not to lambaste someone who has slighted you in your past. Rather, it gives you a chance to show both balanced and thoughtful reflections on ethical issues. And take note—while some schools ask you to present the steps you took to deal with the ethical dilemma you faced, others want only to hear about the problem, not the solution.

CASE STUDY 1

Southern Chemical was a manufacturing organization that used chemical formulations devised by a well-respected research-and-development (R&D) firm. Southern's finished goods would bear the symbol of the R&D firm as a stamp of approval that was recognized throughout the industry. In the course of years of manufacturing refinements, and the use of substitute materials when the specified ones were not available, Southern had modified the formula to such a point that it resembled the patented original only slightly. However, the product still carried the R&D firm's symbol.

As a lab technician, I worked with the formulas on a daily basis. I was uncomfortable with our use of the R&D company's label, and this was worsened by a visit by representatives of the R&D firm during which we were asked to hide inventory of substitute materials and prominently display the specified ones.

I had a close relationship with Southern's vice president and I approached him to discuss the issue. He explained that the formula changes had been kept from the R&D company as protection against their dropping Southern as their primary manufacturer. He reasoned that since our product was so different, we could get a new patent and continue our production. Rather than discussing my personal discomfort, I spoke to him in terms of our potential liability and some of the benefits of a more cooperative relationship with the R&D firm. As a result of our conversation, the VP opened discussions with the R&D company and Southern was able to get their backing on the formula refinements. As I left the firm, a more systematic way of communicating formula changes and improvements and the compensation for them was being discussed.

This essay is short and to the point. The writer lays out the problem in a concise manner and presents the approach he took to attempt to resolve it. This problem-resolution segment is an excellent opportunity to show your capacity for creative thinking: Rather than pushing the ethical problems, this writer raised the legal ones. Thus, he was able to encourage a change of policy without directly accusing his boss of foul play. Admissions committees are interested in seeing how you think, how you approach and resolve delicate issues. The "ethical dilemma" question is an excellent forum in which you can showcase your problem-solving skills.

CASE STUDY 2

In the beginning of fiscal year 1992, I worked on an analysis of the vehicle needs of the Bureau of Maintenance. My responsibility was both to see that the analysis contained accurate budget information and also to act as an intermediary between the Bureau personnel preparing it and OMB.

After reviewing a working draft of the analysis, I felt that, while the budget numbers were accurate, our need for vehicles was overstated. I expressed this view strongly in two meetings with the divisional managers and with our vehicle coordinator (who was preparing the analysis). Although many managers agreed with me, they refused to change the analysis, believing it was the OMB's responsibility to cut the request. Additional complications arose when I learned that the vehicle coordinator had sent a draft to the task force containing false information in a supporting schedule.

My dilemma was whether to report either the false information or the inflated assumptions, or both. I feared jeopardizing my strong working relationship with the task force if I did not reveal my reservations about the assumptions. However, my responsibility was to see that the budget numbers were correct, not to see that the actual projections were reasonable. If I were to raise my concerns with the task force, I would risk losing the trust of all the managers within the Bureau, people upon whom I relied for honest assessments on bigger budget issues.

I decided both to keep my reservations about the projections to myself and to confront the vehicle coordinator, forcing him to correct the false vehicle information in our next draft. In this way, I ensured that the backup information we were providing was factual, even if the projections, which were an interpretation, were overstated. I was certain that OMB would reinterpret the backup information, cutting the projections and beginning a process of negotiation. Such a process, while clearly flawed, is an understood aspect of budget preparation. Inflated projections are no less indefensible than OMB's often arbitrary slashing of projections.

This author, too, scores points here in the way that he exhibits original thinking. Admissions committee members know that you will inevitably be faced with such difficult situations in your future jobs, some of you on a regular basis. In their effort to understand your character and mind better, your readers are generally interested not only in what particular aspects of the encounter did not sit well with you, but also in what actions you took to resolve the issue at hand.

ESSAYS ON LEADERSHIP

High on the list of desirable attributes in MBA candidates is leadership ability or potential. A good number of schools will ask you about your leadership experience in questions such as these:

How would you describe the strengths that you bring to situations requiring leadership? What areas of your leadership competence do you hope will undergo further development? (Harvard)

Describe a significant leadership experience, decision-making challenge, or managerial accomplishment. How did this experience affect your professional/personal development? (UVA)

When deciding how to address this question, keep an open mind, as leadership is not confined to the workplace. The applicant who wrote the following response was a management consultant before returning to business school. Rather than writing about an on-the-job leadership experience, he took a much different tack:

CASE STUDY

Uniting people behind a common goal and then developing a plan to get there are two leadership characteristics I demonstrated in an all-day exercise in "Coping with International Conflict," a course I took my junior year.

One Saturday, the entire class participated in an arms-control negotiation simulation where each person was assigned to a team representing one of the superpowers. The opening positions seemed to preclude any agreement: One country (the United

States) would not sign a treaty without on-site verification, while the other country (the Soviet Union) would not allow it (on-site verification). After preliminary morning meetings, prospects for a treaty were faint as negotiators established their positions and refused to budge. Many students were frustrated and felt like they were wasting their time.

I recognized the impasse, and, when we came back from lunch, I tried to get everyone focused on areas of common ground. Didn't we all want to eliminate the threat of these terrible weapons? And wasn't the money that could be saved much needed elsewhere? Surely there was a way we could achieve our common goals, I said.

The other students agreed, but we still seemed to face irreconcilable differences. To reach an agreement, I realized that—as I learned in the course—we had to examine our *interests*, not positions. I mentally removed myself from the negotiating position of my team and analyzed both countries' interests. The interest of the United States was to ensure that the Soviet Union would not cheat. The interest of the Soviet Union was to make certain that the United States would not learn any of their military secrets. Was there any way to negotiate a treaty where both sets of interests would be met, at least to the degree that the leadership of both countries (the professors and section leaders) would agree to sign it?

I took the lead for my team and began probing the minute details. Would it be acceptable if each country could put monitoring devices outside any buildings it felt might be used for weapons production? What if on-site inspections were done by scientists from neutral countries, with each superpower having veto power over the selection of the scientists? What devices could the inspectors carry? Exactly how much notice would be given before an inspection could take place? After a long afternoon of negotiations, we eventually hammered out a detailed agreement that violated both countries' original *positions*, but met both countries' *interests*. The leadership of both countries agreed to sign our group's treaty, the first time this had ever happened in years of running the exercise.

By uniting everyone behind a common goal and then developing an action plan, I not only learned a tremendous amount, but also attracted the attention of the professors, who asked me to become a section leader in the course the following year. I accepted and assumed full responsibility for preparing and teaching a weekly two-hour section and grading all the students. I was flattered when I later found out that I was the only undergraduate section leader of a liberal arts course at Harvard (in fact, Harvard policy only permits undergraduates to be Teaching Assistants, not Teaching Fellows—as I was—in liberal arts courses because of the subjective nature of the grading, but fortunately for me we discovered this too late).

This author did not limit himself to the work environment, choosing instead to describe an unusual leadership experience from his undergraduate studies. He gives the reader a detailed look at how he took charge and at the results he achieved by leading the other group participants to approach the problem from a new perspective. When writing your response to this sort of question, pick an anecdote that will give the reader a good sense of your leadership style, as this writer has done. In addition, show your audience what you are capable of doing when you are in charge. Strong leadership abilities are crucial to be a good manager. Your readers want to see what you can do in a position of authority.

ESSAYS ON COMMUNITY/EXTRACURRICULAR ACTIVITIES

The questions that address your community or extracurricular activities offer a prime opportunity to present a vivid description of your life outside of work that will differentiate you from your fellow applicants. This type of question appears in many different guises:

List your involvement in community, extracurricular, and professional activities. Please indicate the dates of your involvement, the scope of your responsibilities, whether you were elected or appointed to leadership positions, and the offices held. (University of Chicago)

*What **one** nonprofessional activity do you find most inspirational, and why? (Wharton)*

For fun, I . . . (Kellogg)

Use this question wisely; you have the chance to address intriguing elements of background that won't come out in some of the more standard, work-related questions that you must answer. We provide you with several examples here to illustrate the true range of possibilities these questions present for the enhancement of your application with an engaging discussion of your nonprofessional pursuits.

CASE STUDY 1

I was a founding member of a new national teacher corps, Teach for America. In two short years, Teach for America has recruited, trained, and placed over 1,200 motivated recent college graduates as public school teachers in various areas of the United States that suffer from persistent teacher shortages.

I met Wendy Kopp, the founder, in the fall of my senior year at a conference at Princeton she organized and was impressed with her organizational and leadership skills, as well as her contacts with senior business leaders. When her brother—who didn't realize I knew Wendy—told me about her idea the following spring, I was tremendously excited. At this stage, she hadn't even written her thesis, much less founded the organization or raised a penny, but she was determined to do it and wanted me to help her. I agreed, with the understanding that it would be short-term since I had already committed to a great new job with the Boston Consulting Group (BCG).

Wendy worked over the summer, and four of us joined her in the fall. What an exciting time! All of us had certain areas of responsibility, but everyone worked on everything from early morning to long past midnight. We had numerous spontaneous meetings every day as we developed a strategy for building the organization. I was chief financial officer and set up a system to carefully track our money and budget future expenses. I kept Wendy informed of the day on which we would run out of money if she didn't get more contributions. Rarely did we have more than a two-week window, and, on more than one occasion, Wendy and I had to delay cashing our paychecks until a donation came in.

In addition, I served as office manager. I managed part-time college student workers, evaluated and obtained health benefits and other forms of insurance, maintained relationships with our pro bono law firm, ad agency, design firm, and many other service providers, and developed relationships with people at Morgan Stanley—the company that donated office space to us—that later saved us tens of thousands of dollars in phone, supplies, xeroxing, and printing costs.

Lastly, I played a major role in the Campus Representative conference. We had decided that the best way to attract college students to join Teach for America was through a grassroots effort rather than the traditional approach of using career service offices. The key to this effort was developing a network of one or two students on each of 100 college campuses, who would work to promote Teach for America by getting articles in student publications, holding information sessions, meeting with student leaders of campus organizations, and so on. But how could we get people to volunteer to do this? We decided that we had to recruit people over the phone and invite them to a conference where we could train and motivate them.

For a month, I spent every afternoon and evening on the phone, trying to convince busy college students to devote a great deal of time and energy to a tiny organization that was located in New York and of which they had never heard. Through personal contacts, hundreds of phone calls, and unwavering conviction in a powerful idea, two of us were able to recruit a group of people for the conference. This was only the first step, however. At the same time, I was arranging airfare for 100 people, ordering meals, developing a schedule, attracting publicity (which lead to a *Newsweek* article and a PBS special), and taking care of all the necessary details. The conference was tremendous: None of us got any sleep for a week. But by the time it was over, 160 inspired students went back to their campuses to get their fellow students as excited about Teach for America as all of us were.

Shortly thereafter, Wendy and I discussed my future there. In order to put me in charge of fund-raising or recruitment and selection, Wendy needed a long-term commitment. It was an emotionally wrenching decision for me. Although I loved the organization and believed in it deeply, I was unhappy in New York and excited about the challenges and opportunities that awaited me at BCG. Also, Teach for America was on solid ground, with adequate financing and a staff of 20; so I decided to return home to Boston.

This is the essay we mentioned in Chapter 5, one that provides solid support for the author's positioning as a public-minded entrepreneur. In describing his work with Teach for America, the writer communicates feelings of dedication and passion, attributes that are appealing to admissions officers. The admissions committees are looking for people that approach their activities outside of work with the same sort of vigor and commitment that will make them successful both in a competitive MBA program and in the working world. The writer understands this and communicates a strong sense of energy, interest, and enthusiasm in his account of his activities in the nonprofit sector. This extracurricular/community question will often give you an opportunity to sneak in a bit more information about your leadership abilities. In this example, the writer emphasizes the degree to which he directed and executed tasks that were essential to the success of this start-up educational venture.

CASE STUDY 2

In addition to my work for the City, I feel I have made a contribution over the last three years as a tutor in the Volunteer Services for Children reading program. Once a week, my wife and I tutor in their "Hell's Kitchen" community center for an hour and a half. While the program is officially for reading, we try to focus on those subjects in which our tutees need the most help.

The most recent of my tutees needed help in every course. George had failed all of his subjects but one. Before I was assigned to him, I had been told by the head of the program that he had the potential to be a good student but had been distracted by family problems. His teacher had reported that he had done very little homework in recent months.

I tried to boost George's self-confidence. Math was his best subject and so, if he did not have an upcoming test in another subject, we would work on geometry. I challenged him on problems, getting him not to look in the back of the book before first coming up with an answer. Gradually, George's confidence in his math ability began to increase, and he took to helping out Rachel, my wife's tutee, on her math problems. To spur his interest in learning, I would also have little competitions. He would ask me something, anything, from his American history text, and I would ask him something from one of the chapters he had read. We kept score, and I often made sure that it was close or that he won. One time, my wife, another tutor, and I sponsored a competition: Which tutee could name the most U.S. presidents? Another time, the competition was geography: Who could identify the most states on an outline of a U.S. map?

While these games taught George information that everyone should know, my purpose behind them was to make my time as constructive as possible. I could not tutor George only in his worst subjects—they were all bad. Instead, I had to convince him that learning was fun and that well-educated people were worthy role models. Ultimately, measuring my success will be very hard, but in the short term, the indications are good. George finished his last semester passing every course but one.

Whereas the first case study showed an applicant who tackled an educational issue at the macro-level, this essay shows the impact a person can have through one-on-one interaction with a needy student. The contrast between this and the first case study is worth noting: You don't have to develop a nonprofit from the ground up to make a difference in your community. So don't sell yourself short. If you've focused your efforts on helping one individual, describe what you've done and for whom, as our author has here. An account of your work with a single person may, in fact, be more poignant than an essay that describes a larger-scale community service effort.

CASE STUDY 3

When I'm not working on ads and articles, you can usually find me exploring the outdoors. The San Francisco Bay area is an unusual locale. It is the fourth largest metropolitan area in the country, yet it is unique in providing nature enthusiasts with easy access to a plethora of outdoor activities. My interest in the outdoors is an intense and personal one; the range and diversity of my activities reflect my innate curiosity and my desire to learn about the natural world. A typical weekend might include skin diving for abalone along the Mendocino coast, hunting for pheasants in the rice fields of the Sacramento Valley, or sea kayaking in nearby Richardson Bay. In a region that supports such a wide assortment of ecological habitats, my outdoor adventures are my way of exploring these niches and learning about the flora and fauna they support. They can be a way for me to satisfy my craving for a vigorous physical challenge (mountain biking on Mount Tamalpais) or simply an escape from hectic urban life (a quiet hike in the Golden Gate National Recreation Area). Of course, in an area with a population of 1.5 million people, sometimes it is hard to get away completely; the resulting clash between my rural interests and urban reality has produced some hilarious results. My fiancée and I have attracted tourists' attention down on Fisherman's Wharf as we walked back to our car after an afternoon of crabbing in San Francisco Bay, one of us carrying dripping nets, the other a bucket of skittering, skirmishing rock crabs. And I've received some classic looks from people in my San Francisco neighborhood after returning from a morning hunt, sauntering up Sacramento Street in my blaze orange vest, clutching a pair of pheasants by their skinny red ankles. Images such as these might raise no eyebrows whatsoever in other parts of the country—I hope I get there someday. But for now, I feel lucky to be in a location that provides me excellent professional opportunities, as well as the chance for the outdoor adventures that are so important to me.

The first two essays in this category covered community activities. As a contrast, we thought it was important to also include an essay that describes other hobbies. Just as we saw in the two prior samples, the author communicates a passion for his pastimes—in this case, outdoor adventures. His writing is colorful, and he successfully uses creative language and imagery to paint brilliant pictures of his outdoor escapades in the minds of the reader. Given the enormous volume of applications that admissions committee members must review, it makes good sense to use language that will capture their attention and leave them with lasting visual images.

ESSAY ON A MENTOR

Admissions officers can learn a lot about your professional development through your description of your mentors. This type of question will read something like the following:

Describe the characteristics of an exceptional manager using an example of someone whom you have observed or with whom you have worked. Illustrate how his or her management style has influenced you. (Tuck)

CASE STUDY

There have been two managers who have had a significant impact on my personal and professional development; each has played a major role in a specific period of my life. As a neophyte to Salomon Brothers Inc, I was first introduced to my direct manager, Martin Green, who was to serve as the bane of my existence in the fast-paced, wheelin' dealin' world of investment banking. Despite Martin's insipid character, he was an exceptional manager. In contrast, George Keyser, one of my managers in the management consulting practice for Information Technology at Deloitte & Touche, is an exceptional manager and also an amiable human being.

Admittedly, I despised Martin, yet I respected him immensely. In my early days at Salomon, I was dubbed "Mary Poppins." Enough said. Martin promised to "toughen me up." Indeed, Martin was exceptional. He was bright; we all respected his intelligence and business acumen. In addition to his knowledge about the financial world, Martin was an excellent mentor. Moderately patient, he enjoyed teaching me about interest rates, bonds, yields, LBOs (leveraged buyouts), and other financial models. For a year, he quizzed me daily, "What is prime today?" For the first three months, in anticipation of his spontaneous, often sardonic questions, my keyboard quivered when he approached. Martin exhibited another trait that I could not help but admire: He never asked me to do anything that he would not do himself. Martin was one of the few vice presidents who could actually execute a comparables work sheet alone and was also one of a select group who would grunt with the analysts until 3 A.M. At the same time, he could also grasp the broader view of a situation and concoct business solutions instantly. He constantly reminded me that I was "living the dream." What Martin perceived as a "dream" was actually excruciating attention to detail and insane nights of human endurance. Why did I stay? Martin is part of the answer. While I detested his tortuous method of teaching, he did motivate me as a good manager should. He was able to pull at my innate desire to excel; he cultivated my desire to learn. From the incredible "dream," I have been able to retain and maintain my perverted attention to detail, analytical skills, and a tougher, perhaps more experienced exterior.

In sharp contrast to Martin, I actually liked George Keyser. He served as my manager for an expert-systems project at Deloitte & Touche. At the time I began as a consultant at Deloitte, I was seeking an environment with less supervision. I had been thoroughly grounded in the rules of the workplace and needed autonomy. George was the perfect macromanager. Very broad-minded, he had the ability to grasp the business implications of the project, while he could also answer the most detailed system-related question. Like Martin, George is an expert in his field. He can answer almost any question regarding information systems, and what he does not know, he will find out. Through George, I discovered the wonders and intricacies of terminal emulation. In addition, George exhibited another trait indicative of a strong manager: He delegated authority. Despite the fact that I had just learned the definition of *terminal emulation*, he gave me the responsibility of writing the specifications for the terminal-emulation program. That was motivation. The responsibility, ownership, and power to succeed or fail were intense motivating factors. With all of the project members, he emphasized the aspect of teamwork and the need to constantly interact with one another. He reminded us that "It's like a tug of war. If we all pull together, we can succeed. If we all pull at different times, we'll fall flat on our faces." Above all else, George is enjoyable to work with. He possesses an excellent sense of humor, a powerful tool for disarming conflict and building bonds with people. Using his interpersonal skills, he is able to cultivate trust and respect with clients and with his team members. From him, I have learned that one can respect, enjoy, and like a good manager.

The comparison of two strikingly different managers proves to be an effective technique here. Despite the dissimilar nature of the two, both are good managers and taught the applicant important lessons. In writing your essay on the issue, be concrete. What did your mentor teach you and how? What elements of his or her managerial style have you absorbed, and which have you rejected? How might these lessons strengthen the elements of your background that you highlight in your personal positioning? Admissions staffers are interested in seeing not only what you have learned, but the kind of people from whom you learn. This essay proves that the writer is capable of learning from a broad spectrum of people; she takes the best bits of managerial wisdom from different people and includes them in her own portfolio of skills.

ESSAYS ON STRENGTHS AND WEAKNESSES

Questions about personal strengths and weaknesses are standard fare in job interviews. Variations on this same question type now appear in MBA applications on a regular basis:

What character traits do you consider your strengths? (HBS)

I disappoint myself when I am _____. (Kellogg)

CASE STUDY 1

One of my best character traits is that I am able to work well with many different types of people. For example, while developing software at Apple Computer, I had to work with someone who was generally considered to be a moody naysayer. Present an idea to Jennifer and it would be shot down with a flurry of objections and delays; thus, most engineers tried to avoid her. I was in a position where I could not work around her.

In discreet conversations with others, I began to recognize that Jennifer said no when others demanded an immediate yes. She needed time for reflection when others, done with their review, expected rapid agreement. I found that if I stretched things out, gave her time to think, she would accept ideas even more enthusiastically than other members of the team! We worked perfectly together because I was able to accommodate her diversity.

My other strengths are creativity and resourcefulness. From creating Halloween haunted houses as a kid to slipping "sexy" new features into my software, I often come up with new and unique ideas and have the wherewithal and organizational skills necessary to make those ideas come alive.

This essay succeeds by offering anecdotes that support the writer's assertions concerning his strengths. Beware unsupported platitudes! All too frequently, applicants make broad, general statements about their personal strengths with little evidence to back them up. To make your positioning real, give the reader solid, specific examples that support your claims.

CASE STUDY 2

My brother tells me that my indecisiveness stems from the fact I was born a Gemini—one person with two minds. Geminis are notorious for putting off a decision until the last possible moment, methodically weighing every variable. Indeed, I do have the tendency to be indecisive if I know an immediate decision is not needed. However, once I make a decision, I will maintain a commitment to that decision unless the circumstances change. And I am not hesitant to voice my opinions and my supporting reasons.

In general, I am a good decision maker. I logically analyze every alternative before drawing conclusions. At work, I gather as much hard data as is available before analyzing all the options, whether I am working on a business strategy or a system design. Because I am able to think clearly and logically, my analysis and decisions are respected. In my personal life as well, I am generally looked to by my friends for group decisions—such as what restaurant to eat at or what movie to watch. However, there are decisions, such as my resolution to leave Bain, that I will agonize over, creating a pros/cons list, soliciting opinions, and analyzing all the variables multiple times before reaching a conclusion. If a decision has no pending deadline, I will procrastinate until the drop-dead date; this can be a showstopper for others who are dependent on my decision. To ensure good decisions and prod myself into making decisions before a deadline, I religiously record due dates in my calendar and mount yellow Post-its on my computer. And all this because I was born in May.

In crafting a "weaknesses" essay, step one is to address a shortcoming that is, in fact, a real weakness. As you will read in our interviews with admissions directors in Chapter 12, insipid statements such as "I work too hard," in which you attempt to couch a strength in the language of inadequacy, will fail. Be honest and grapple with what you feel is a true personal-character flaw or two. Again, as you did when categorizing your strengths, give examples. But for your essay to be truly effective, you need not only to write candidly about your imperfections, but also to discuss how you address them. In this sample, our writer covers some of the techniques she uses to overcome her tendency to procrastinate. Bonus points go to applicants who can indicate how specific elements of the MBA training would help them to conquer their faults.

OPTIONAL ESSAYS

Many of the applications you will receive will give you the opportunity to go beyond the basic format they prescribe with "optional" essay questions that read like these:

> *What would you like for the Admissions Committee to know about you, that might not be apparent through the materials in your file, before we make a decision? (Duke University's Fuqua School of Business)*

> *What else would you like to share with the Admissions Committee that is not presented elsewhere in your application? If you feel that your credentials and application represent you fully, then do not feel obligated to write anything more. (Wharton)*

The second sentence of the Wharton question seems ridiculous. If you've managed to capture the subtleties of your entire life in four essay questions, a transcript, and a couple of recommendations, then there must not be much to talk about in the first place. You undoubtedly have more information to share that will further strengthen your case. Take this chance to move beyond the rigid structure you've been forced to use until now and deepen your readers' understanding of who you are.

CASE STUDY 1

Over the past three years, a relationship that began senior year with a zany evening at a "Gilligan's Island" theme party has grown into a loving, thriving partnership. Through Jennifer Wu, my Chinese-American fiancée (and fellow UCLA applicant), I've been fortunate enough to get an exceptional exposure to a vibrant culture, gaining an insider's view that has included everything from a liberal dosage of Chinese political philosophy to evenings of jiao-tzu (steamed dumplings) and raw garlic shared with Jennifer's non-English-speaking relatives. As a partner in an interracial relationship, I have faced challenges that I had never expected would be a part of my life. From intricate family politics to outright discrimination, I have grappled with the presence and pain of issues I had never dealt with in my personal or public life. But despite the complexities I have found to be an integral part of an interracial relationship, I feel that the emotional and intellectual rewards of this kind of partnership are innumerable. Through Jennifer, I have learned of endurance and respect, selflessness and love. I have come to reevaluate ideas and institutions I never questioned in the past, to see things through the eyes of another. And I have gained a unique understanding of Chinese culture that I could have never gained without such an adventurous teacher.

The challenges that we have faced as an interracial couple have been many and varied. Some have been within our own families. Jennifer's grandparents have been surprised with her choice of a Caucasian partner and have been slow to accept me. Although Jennifer and I are engaged and have been seeing each other for almost three years, it was not until last week that Jennifer's grandfather asked her what my name was. Her parents' traditional values have put us in a sticky situation or two as well—try explaining the concept of "living together" to a conservative Chinese family, and you'll know exactly what I mean. And we certainly took *my* family by surprise when we told them we planned to hold a traditional 13-course Chinese banquet the evening of our forthcoming June wedding. In our public lives, as a couple, we have faced bias and prejudice that has ranged from subtle to blatant. The two of us recently had dinner at a Chinese restaurant where, although he spoke perfect English, the waiter spoke only to Jennifer, barely acknowledging my presence. While walking through San Francisco's theater district, we ran into a group of skinheads who threw a Coke can at me and repeatedly called Jennifer "chink."

Episodes like these have been discouraging. But the strength of the relationship we have formed and the amount I have learned from Jennifer makes these issues pale in comparison. In her book *Legacies: A Chinese Mosaic*, Bette Bao Lord wrote, "All throughout their long history, Chinese have prized . . . a quality which has been elevated to a cardinal virtue, *ren*. The dictionary translation is 'to endure.' But more telling than the English definition is the ideogram: the cutting edge of a sword above a heart." Jennifer is a determined woman who has taught me much about endurance. In our first year out of Stanford, both of us had positions as financial analysts in which we worked extremely long hours. Jennifer's attitude of perseverance had a strong effect on me and helped the two of us to keep our relationship together and to weather a difficult transition between life as students and life as working professionals. She has shown me that a bit of respect for one's elders can work wonders—I recently shot up a notch or two in the eyes of her grandparents when I brought them a duck (webbed feet and all!) after a successful day of duck hunting. Jennifer has also taught me of selflessness and love, two qualities that are intimately interwoven in our relationship. We have come to live our lives as partners, helping one another in ways big and small and sharing our thoughts, our feelings, and our aspirations in a way I never knew I could.

Just as my emotional life has flourished in this unique relationship, so has my mind. Our discussion, debate, and banter have often prodded me to look at issues from a new perspective. What role should affirmative action play in the workplace, if any? How can universities best expose undergraduates to material beyond the standard "Western Culture" core? We often come at such issues from different angles; our own "personal dialectic" is thought-provoking for us both. Our interracial relationship has provided me with a unique window on the world of Chinese politics, mores, and culture. Talks with Jennifer's father, a professor of political science, have shown me a view of the communist revolution from a man who was forced to flee his country with the coming of the Red Army. Living day to day with Jennifer provides constant insight into Chinese values. And raucous dinners with her extended family have shown me a culture that is generous and jovial, friendly and forgiving. We have faced challenges thus far, Jennifer and I. No doubt many more will come our way. But in the spirit of *ren*, we shall endure, for the pleasure is clearly worth the pain.

The degree of insight an admissions committee gains about the writer through this poignant essay goes way beyond what could be learned through the more standard application material. The writer's description of his interracial relationship and its rich and varied effects on his life present an entirely different side of his persona than would appear in a description of his "three greatest accomplishments." To give your reader a more complex, intriguing picture of yourself, make the extra effort: Don't skip an essay that has been deceptively labeled as "optional."

CASE STUDY 2

An old Chinese man moves in slow motion with his eyes closed as the sun rises. He performs different standard movements in which he caresses an invisible ball or stands like a bird. He practices tai ji quan, a traditional slow-motion martial art of China. As the world awakens, the old man finishes his exercise and heads home. He walks with the energy of a youngster and smiles. This traditional art works for him. His experience explains why I find tai ji quan my most inspirational nonprofessional activity. It helps my mental and physical health and deepens my cross-cultural experience in China.

Tai ji quan exercises both my mental and physical faculties. It focuses my mind completely on my breathing and body movement. When I perform this martial art, I lose awareness of everything outside of myself. Breathing in harmony with each movement of my body represents the goal. Learning to do this takes much practice, but it rewards me. As I harmonize my breathing and body, I move beyond myself and feel in harmony with the air and the earth. A peace of mind results that I fail to find in other activities. Also, tai ji quan increases my awareness and my control of my physical movement. Moving my body endlessly in standard slow-motion routines makes me aware of the subtleties of body movement. It also practices my control of that movement to a greater extent than any other exercise. I notice this increased awareness and control of physical movement when I pick up a cup, walk, or play basketball. In the end, I know this activity helps me simply because I feel mentally and physically healthier.

This martial art inspires me most because it deepens my cross-cultural experience by acquainting me with a traditional Chinese art and another side of the teacher-student relationship of Chinese culture. Millions of Chinese practice tai ji quan daily, as people have for centuries. Participation helps me to understand why. It offers another way to learn about China through a Chinese art. Not only do I learn tai ji quan but also about the teacher-student relationship. I better understand the student's perspective on the relationship because of my interaction with my tai ji quan instructor. For instance, as a traditional leader, he accepts no pay. I learned that seeing the traditions of this art passed on provides its own payment. However, I also discovered that, as his student, I should offer whatever gifts I can. That explains why I tutor him in English. This relationship gives me additional insight into the culture that I might not otherwise uncover.

These mental, physical, and cross-cultural benefits explain why tai ji quan inspires me. I see myself as an old Chinese man practicing this traditional art in a hopeful vision of my future.

This essay was written by the same friend who spent time living and teaching in China (see page 83). Learning tai ji quan was an important aspect of his two-year experience there, and he continues to practice the art now that he has returned to the United States. It provides, he says, a moment of calm in the midst of his otherwise hectic life as a first-year business school student.

As both this essay and the preceding one illustrate, you should not feel restrained to writing about your professional or academic life in the "optional" essay. Given the structure of the average application, it's more than likely that you've been forced to spend the majority of your application writing about those elements of your background. Use this essay to provide the admissions committee with another perspective on your character and to broaden their understanding of who you are and what is important to you. The tai ji quan essay does exactly that, reinforcing the applicant's positioning. The writer gives the admissions officers added insight concerning his experience in China and some of the benefits that this two year detour from the standard pre-MBA career path provided for him. While it is certain that the Wharton admissions committee saw plenty of applications from candidates who had spent time in the banking industry, it is unlikely that many of these bankers left their comfortable lives in the United States in exchange for two years in a third world country at a fraction of their former salary. This applicant's experiences are intriguing and set him apart from the crowd. Using the optional essay to drive this point home is a wise choice.

EXTRAS

As you assemble your applications, you may feel the occasional drive to include a bit of extra material. Be judicious here; admissions committees don't have the time or patience to watch videotapes, for example, of your dramatic premiere in a community theater production of *Fiddler on the Roof*. But if you have a photograph, an article you've written, or another extra that you think furthers your case, include it—along with a brief note of explanation.

CASE STUDY 1: ASIAN TERMINAL EMULATOR
AND PROBEVIEW SNAPSHOTS

To give you a better idea of what the products I have developed look like, I have attached printouts of typical screens. The first picture comes from the UNIX-IBM Asian terminal emulator that I worked on in 1988 and 1989. A Japanese-, Chinese-, or Korean-speaking person can use a terminal attached to an HP (Hewlett-Packard) UNIX computer to connect to an IBM mainframe where they can read electronic mail, run an inventory program, and so on, and see all of this information displayed to them in their native language. They can also type in English and Asian characters from the keyboard.

HP is an international company (more than half of its revenues are derived outside of the United States) and it believes that building products that work in languages other than English is a necessary key to its success. This product was the first networking product to run with Asian languages and has provided HP with an important competitive advantage in Asia.

The second printout is from ProbeView, the distributed network management software I have helped create. Node Traffic is a new part of ProbeView that collects information about who is talking on the network. It lets a network manager figure out that John's PC is talking too much while Mary's PC is sending too many errors onto the network, among other things.

The attached article from a recent issue of *PC Week* includes one user's opinion of Node Traffic and also mentions AutoPolling, the feature that I helped keep from being cut from the product when one of the two engineers originally assigned to AutoPolling quit and the other left on temporary disability leave.

Screen printouts make good sense here. The average admissions committee member is unlikely to have a degree in computer science, and visual representations of the product the applicant describes in the essay will give the reader a better understanding of what the applicant has been up to at Hewlett-Packard.

CASE STUDY 2: A BRIEF NOTE

I have included three recommendations for your review with my application. Each of these recommenders knows me in a different capacity and, thus, has a unique perspective on my academic and professional capabilities. The first of these is George Stevens, President of E-Star Systems and my manager for the past year and a half. George has been extremely influential in my development as a high-technology marketer and has taught me a great deal about the complexities of the software industry. The second is Jody Minsky, Professor of Art History at Stanford University. I spent two quarters with Jody studying the art of the ancient Greeks; Jody is familiar with my enthusiasm for the academic environment and has seen me excel within a unique academic niche. The third recommender is Bob Rodriguez, a professor at the Stanford University School of Law. Bob is a mentor and a friend, someone who has known me since I was young. He has seen me develop over time as a person, a student, and a professional, and his advice along the way has been invaluable. Bob has a "long-term" understanding of my character that can only come with time; I think you will find his comments to be insightful and informative. If you have questions for any of these three individuals, please feel free to give them a call.

Best regards,

Phil Carpenter

If you're going to include additional recommendations, it is a good idea to explain why. As Phil did, let your readers know who your recommenders are, how they know you, and what perspectives they offer on your character, academic performance, or work experience.

9

Interviews: The Inside Story

Words are, of course, the most powerful drug used by mankind.

RUDYARD KIPLING
Speech, February 14, 1923

The interview is becoming an increasingly important part of the MBA application process. While Kellogg and Carnegie Mellon are still the only top-tier schools that require all of their applicants to interview, a growing number of schools are pushing to interview a greater percentage of their total applicant pool than they have in the past. Admissions committees have realized that there are valuable things to be learned in these encounters.

This chapter gives you background information to prepare you for your interviews as well as our recommendations on how to use them to your advantage. It also provides you with advice and suggestions on the interview process from admissions directors, alumni, and current students—the very people who will be on the other side of the desk during your interviews.

THE NATURE OF THE BEAST

The basic details of the interview process are as follows:

What

The MBA interview is generally a 30- to 60-minute session that enables schools to get a glimpse of the person behind the paper. It carries different degrees of weight from school to school, and MBA programs make use of the interview in varying degrees. While Kellogg may be at one extreme, interviewing all those who apply, Stanford is at the other: The school does not conduct any interviews. Harvard takes a hybrid approach: If its admissions officers want to talk to you (perhaps they feel they need more information about certain elements of your background), they'll let you know, but you cannot request an interview. You can find out more about the role that the interview plays in a particular school's admissions process when you call to request an application.

Think of the interview as a sales call. It's your chance for some face-to-face selling, one of the most effective sales techniques around. You have an extraordinary opportunity to present your message to your customer, to explain how your "product" is different from competitive offerings, and to address any objections or questions the customer may have in real time. Our goal in this chapter is to prepare you to take full advantage of this face-to-face encounter with a highly selective buyer.

Who

As was mentioned, in each interview, you'll be meeting with a member of the admissions committee, an alumnus, or a current student. The character of your interview can be quite different according to the stakeholder group your interviewer represents. An admissions officer is likely to be pleasant but efficient, to push you to varying degrees according to that person's level of seniority within the admissions hierarchy, and to hold the party line on difficult issues. A student can be more casual and is less likely to care about being politically correct. Ask him or her a tough question and you're likely to get a straight answer. However, students can also push you more on tricky or delicate subjects. After all, they are making a serious investment of time and money in their school; they have a vested interest in ensuring that students that follow them are top-notch.

Alumni can be the biggest wild card of all in the interview process. Of course, schools attempt to find alumni who they think are good ambassadors, individuals who will provide them with good input for the admissions process and who will be strong spokespeople for the institution. You may find interviews with alumni to be a wonderful experience. Alumni see fewer applicants than do the members of the admissions staff and can afford to take more time to talk to you. An alumnus may provide you with insight not only about the program itself, but also about the value of the education and reputation of that school in the real world. They also may take more time to write up their thoughts after the interview and to make a well-presented written argument on your behalf. Of course, despite schools' best efforts at quality control, they make mistakes on occasion in their selection of alumni interviewers. We had a friend who had a horrible interview for Harvard with an alumnus. The man grilled her for three hours, demanding to know, for example, how familiar she was with the works of Kant and Plato. What this has to do with business school, we have no idea; but, after her story, we were terrified that we might find ourselves in a similar situation. Alumni interviews like this are the exception, rather than the standard. However, we believe that it pays to know that the quality of the alumni interview experience has greater potential for variation—on the positive or negative side of the spectrum—than does an interview on campus.

Where

If you are interviewing with an admissions officer, you most likely will do so on campus. Doing an on-campus interview can be a revelation. As you sit in the waiting room with scads of other nervous applicants sporting their best interview duds, you'll realize that you are only one of thousands of applicants whom the program will encounter during the application season. Many schools run their interview programs with frightening efficiency. At Kellogg, we felt like goods on a manufacturing plant's assembly line. While our respective interviewers were both quite friendly, when our half hour was up, they wrapped up the discussions immediately, shook hands, and ushered in the next candidates.

An interview with an admissions official can also take place in your home city. Many of the top MBA programs send representatives of their admissions staff on tour each fall to cities across the country. We interviewed with a woman from Dartmouth's Tuck School, for example, at a hotel in San Francisco. Applicants who applied for entrance to Wharton in 1995 were able to meet with admissions committee members in Atlanta, Miami, Minneapolis, San Francisco, and Seattle. Again, these interviews are short and structured; the Tuck representative definitely kept her eye on the clock. But this option is a great way for you to meet a member of the admissions staff in person without spending the time or money to travel to campus.

When

With respect to timing, we recommend that you complete an application before doing your interview at the school. Writing your application will help you crystallize your thoughts and refine your personal positioning strategy. Doing so before you step into an interview is some of the best preparation you can do. In addition, having written the application, you'll know what you had the opportunity and space to say about yourself and what you had to omit. As a result, you can use some of the time in the interview to go beyond the content of your written application, to discuss aspects of your background that you want to communicate to the admissions staff but didn't have a chance to include on paper.

SUGGESTIONS FOR SUCCESS

Now that you are familiar with some of the basic interview issues, we'd like to share our thoughts with you concerning strategies for interview success.

Schedule Your Interviews ASAP

Although already mentioned in Chapter 3, this point is important enough that we want to reemphasize it here. There are plenty of your peers who will also be looking to interview. Even when interviewing applicants every day, each school's capacity to conduct interviews is limited, and demand is greater than supply. As a result, it is essential for you to set up your interviews as soon as possible. If you can do this in September, so much the better. Phil remembers sitting in the Wharton waiting room in the first week of November and hearing a receptionist tell a prospective applicant who called to schedule an interview that he would have to wait for months if he were interested in interviewing on campus. Avoid the crush—act early.

Setting up interviews early in the season will also give you the luxury of choosing which schools you talk to when. We recommend that you interview with the schools that are less important to you first. This will give you a chance to get used to the MBA interview process and to fine-tune your spiel.

Be Prepared

Sounds blindingly obvious, doesn't it? Yet, as you'll read in the interviewers' discussions that follow, it is extraordinary how often applicants walk into an interview ill-prepared for the discussion. Would a sales representative ever appear at a customer site without knowing his product line well and having spent the time to learn about the distinctive aspects of his customer's business? Certainly not if he were interested in closing the sale. This is one of the more important sales calls you will make in your near future. Be ready for it!

To prepare, begin by reviewing your resume (bring a copy with you to each interview). Be prepared to talk about any and all aspects of your professional, personal, and academic history. Next, put to work the market-research information that you gathered, and be sure that you know what a specific school is offering, that you understand what sets it apart from other MBA programs and how your skills and interests match its strengths. Finally, be ready to ask questions. If you've done your market research well, we're sure you'll have plenty; so be sure to ask them. Interviewers respect candidates who have taken the time to formulate insightful questions about the schools they represent.

As part of your preparation, you may want to run through some practice interviews. If you can recruit someone who has been to business school and knows the pertinent issues, ask him or her to help you. But if you can't rustle up a B-school grad, you can still get good practice by having a friend ask you a list of questions that you've prepared, as it will help you get used to talking out loud about your interest in business school.

Dress Professionally

A bit of sartorial advice: Consider this interview to be of the same caliber as a job interview. Jeans and a sweatshirt won't do. Dress appropriately: Men should wear suits; women should wear suits or similar professional attire. You'll look sharp, you'll feel good about yourself, and you'll make a good impression.

Watch the Clock

You may have only half an hour or so to get your major points across. In the beginning of the interview, ask how much time you'll have and gauge yourself accordingly. Be surreptitious about it, but keep an eye on your watch. You don't want to find yourself running out of time before you've had a chance to discuss several crucial elements of your background.

Strive for an Informational Balance

The interview gives you the chance not only to reinforce the points you make in your written application, but also to bring up some issues that you may not have had the space to address in your essays. When you are interviewed, it is highly likely that the interviewer has not yet read your application. In some cases, he never will, as schools have different policies with respect to student and alumni interviewers reviewing applicants' essays. As a result, when you begin the interview, you have some groundwork to lay. You need to take the time to communicate to the interviewer the main points about your professional, academic, and personal background that you convey in your written application. This material, after all, is the foundation of your personal marketing campaign. Nonetheless, you also want to take advantage of this opportunity to include new bits of information, information not included in your essays but that supports your personal positioning and helps the interviewer to understand in greater depth how you are different from other applicants. Managing this informational balance can be a challenge, especially in the limited time you may have available. The important thing, however, is to realize that you are aiming to leave your interviewer with more information about you than he would have by simply reading your essays. Where it's possible, give 110 percent.

Visuals

You may want to consider bringing to the interview something tangible that helps illustrate visually a subject that you discuss in your application. Phil, for example, brought a small portfolio with him in which he had copies of some of the advertisements and direct-mail pieces he had worked on as the marketing manager of a small software company. These helped interviewers to get a better understanding of certain important elements of his job. Be reasonable: If you were an engineer at GE, for example, we wouldn't recommend lugging the microwave oven you helped design through the front door of UCLA's admissions office. But you may well want to bring a picture of it, as this would enable your interviewer to see the results of your hard work and might help him or her to remember you better.

Develop a Dialogue

Remember that these interviews should be a dialogue, not an interrogation. Don't be passive. Feel free to ask questions where appropriate and to turn the conversation gently where necessary to ensure that you cover subjects that you feel to be important in the course of the interview period. In the next section, we'll give you suggestions on how to steer the conversation. But be sensitive here—you don't want to dominate the session. Your interviewers have issues they want to explore with you and questions they want to ask you; you don't want to appear as if you are wedded to your own agenda. Ideally, the interview should be a conversation, an open exchange of information, ideas, and opinions. Rather than simply answering the questions that are asked, engage the interviewer. Both you and your interviewer will enjoy the session much more if it is a dialogue, not a monologue; so go ahead and speak up.

Provide Direction Where Necessary

If you feel like the conversation isn't going where you'd like, give it a nudge. There are several devices you can use to direct the interview toward subjects you'd like to cover:

The Hook

With a hook, you influence the next question that will be asked by ending your message with an intriguing statement. A hook will prompt the interviewer to ask a follow-up question that you want to answer:

EXAMPLES

"That's probably my second most significant achievement." (What was the first?)
"I took some unusual steps to motivate members of our project team." (What did you do?)

The Bridge

A bridge is a phrase that helps you to transition from one issue or question to another. The bridge helps you to shift the conversation to address a subject you want to cover.

EXAMPLES

"That may be true, but it's also worth noting that . . ."
"I'm not sure whether I want to return to consulting after business school, but I do know that . . ."

Simple tools like these can enable you to steer your interview toward a subject you want to discuss in the brief time you've been allotted to make your case. They also can help you to avoid dangerous subjects. If you are asked a question you don't want to answer in detail, give an abbreviated answer and use a bridge to shift to an issue that you feel more confident addressing.

Follow Up

After the interview, send your interviewer a thank you note. This is a courteous gesture, and it's also one more chance for you to get in front of your customer. Alumni and students are not paid to conduct these interviews. They do them as a goodwill gesture, as a way of giving something back to a school that has meant something important to them. You should recognize this by thanking them for their time.

SAMPLE QUESTIONS

In preparation for your interview, run through the following questions, categorized according to topic. Can you articulate cohesive responses to these questions? Which are the most difficult for you to answer? Why? If you are having trouble with certain questions, think them through until you have answers you would feel comfortable giving. Practicing answering these questions, either by yourself or with a friend, will get you in the right mind-set for the interview process.

Character

- If you were a brand, what brand would it be and why?
- How would your friends describe you?
- What have you done that you are proud of?

Academic/Professional

- Why did you attend College X?
- Why did you major in X?
- What scores did you get on the GMAT? The SAT?
- Describe an awkward situation you encountered in managing a subordinate.
- What led you to work at company X?
- Who are your company's customers?
- What do you like best about your current job?

Extracurricular

- What groups were you involved with at college and what did you do in them?
- What community service work have you done lately?
- What are you involved with besides work?

Business School

- Why do you want to go to business school now?
- Why do you want to attend this school?
- Is there a particular area of study in which you plan to concentrate?
- What *specific* questions do you have about our school?

- Why should I believe that you truly want to be a general manager and don't plan on going into consulting or investment banking?
- What do you see yourself doing in five (ten) years?

A GLIMPSE OF REALITY

To show you how those on the other side of the desk think about various interview-related issues, we talked to a number of representatives of different schools who are involved in the interview process. They include:

Admissions Directors

- Henry Malin, Tuck/Dartmouth College
- Melinda Bissett, Fuqua/Duke University

Alumni

- Michael Numamoto, Kellogg/Northwestern University
- Jeremy Jonas, Wharton/University of Pennsylvania

Students

- Mark Morris, University of Chicago
- Martin Illner, Columbia University

Reading these interviews should help you to get an insider's perspective on the realities of the MBA interview process.

1. What kind of information will an interview give you that you will not get from an applicant's essays?

Henry   The interview helps us get to the information behind the paper: Who is this person for real? How good a presenter is he? What motivates him, what drives him? Is he an aggressive person? Is he a more passive person? You can make yourself look like whatever you think the admissions office wants you to look like on paper, but I think that it is a bit harder to do that in person.

   We do quite a bit of interviewing. It's not only to see who it is who gets the magical spots, but also to determine who is not a good match for the school. In most cases, the interview confirms what we see on paper, rather than directly contradicting it or giving an entirely new direction to the file.

Melinda   I think that you get the whole person. You see everything that they do—their actions, their nonverbals, their presentation—things that you don't get in an essay. In an interview, you can ask things you might not pick up even if the application had ten essays. You can also make it a little bit more personal.

Michael   The interview exposes you to those intangibles—personality, a candidate's interpersonal skills, eye contact, sense of humor, etc. It tells you what type of person you're getting—how she thinks and analyzes situations, what kind of value system she has, and how developed her team and leadership skills are.

Jeremy   The foremost area will be a sense of interpersonal skills. These skills will be important for a candidate's success both in the program and beyond. Today's managers need better cross-functional communication skills and must be adept at working with other people.

Just as important is the opportunity to get a sense of a candidate's leadership skills. That's particularly true for Wharton. When you talk to somebody, it gives you the chance to get a better sense of the track record of leadership he might have put down on paper.

Mark   In an interview, I think that it is hard for someone to hide behind canned answers, something that is easy to do on paper. When you ask someone a point blank question in person, there is nowhere for him or her to run.

You'll also get a sense of the interviewee's basic social skills. If applicants don't look you in the eye when they talk or if they don't shake your hand, you may question what they would be like as part of a team.

Martin   The first thing that comes to mind is presentation. Are they slouching in their seat or are they sitting up straight and alert? Are they neat? Grooming, how they carry themselves, and the like reflect self-confidence and maturity.

If applicants are exaggerating or making things up, it's much easier to tell that in person. In addition, when people are filling out essays, they have the time to think about what they are going to write. As a result, you don't see how well they deal with an unexpected question, how they react to stress, or how they react to new situations. In an interview, you see how they respond to things they don't expect.

2. Do you feel that interviewing gives applicants a competitive advantage in the application process?

Henry   At Tuck, we strongly recommend the interview. The percentage of people who are admitted who were interviewed is in the mid 80s. The raw numbers, then, make a good argument in favor of the interview. The interview gives the applicant a second opportunity to present. It also gives him the advantage of having met someone who is then able to serve as an advocate for his application, a person who is actually sitting there when the decision is being made and who may say, "Yes, that guy's GMAT is not as good as this other applicant's, but I liked him a lot more. Let me tell you why."

Melinda   It does here. If we're down to the last space in the class and have people who have similar profiles, I'm going to admit someone who came for the interview, because that person demonstrated the interest and the commitment to come meet with us. There are a lot more "knowns" about someone who interviewed than the person who did not.

Michael   Yes and no. I would say that for a certain group of people, it gives them a competitive advantage, while for the other group, it gives the school the advantage (see next question). As Kellogg requires an interview of every applicant, there really is no advantage one way or another. For programs that have optional interviews, there can be advantages for some groups of people.

Jeremy   I think that there is a dichotomy between those people for whom there is a real risk of not delivering in an interview and those people who just blow you away, people with a lot of natural confidence who sit there and show you in person the substance that they've already described on paper. It's a high risk situation in which, if you're a solid candidate already, it's going to help you a lot, whereas if you're not a solid candidate, it may work against you. That's a bizarre irony. Not being a good candidate, you might have hoped that this was the one situation that could have helped you out. There are some people who can turn it around, but I would say that maybe it's even dangerous to interview if you're not confident about your likely performance.

When I was a student at Wharton, I also interviewed applicants. I remember several situations then in which, having interviewed someone and having been through the application on paper, I was less favorably disposed to the individual after the interview.

Students need to understand that it is important to package and market oneself carefully. You can do that sight unseen as you labor over your application—some people work on these things for months—but it's much harder to do in a spontaneous laboratory like an interview.

Mark   I don't think interviewing gives you a *big* advantage, unless you think you can really sell yourself. The interview will help you to decide if the school you are visiting is really the school you want to attend, as you'll be meeting people there and, frankly, you'll be interviewing them as much as they'll be evaluating you.

I don't think you can dramatically shift your position with the interview. In fact, the interview evaluation is usually the last thing that's reviewed in the application review process at Chicago. If the reader's and the interviewer's views on an applicant were radically different, it might prompt the reader to go back and reevaluate the application. But, more than likely, by the time of the interview, you are probably well on your way to "accept" or "deny."

Martin   For those who are forthright, present themselves well, and demonstrate their ability to deal with the unexpected, it absolutely gives them an advantage. Frankly, I would also say that an attractive applicant, male or female, or one who is very presentable, very personable, also has a definite advantage in an interview. I run into some applicants who don't come across well through test scores or through grades, yet, in person, are charming, witty, and have the right word for every situation. These qualities are important elements of their personalities and come out in the interview.

3. What kind of personalities do you think are best suited for the interview process? Who would you counsel to avoid the interview if possible?

Henry   I think I wouldn't stereotype one kind of person as being the best fit. Someone should come into an interview ready to sell himself. He should have thought about the question "Why do I want an MBA?" before it's asked and should have an answer for that question. He should have an answer for why he selected a specific college, how he chose to work for a particular company, and other choices he has made along the way. People who have done this preparation, regardless of personality, are going to do fine in an interview. I think that the people who should avoid an interview are those who, in person, are going to cast such a negative shadow over the rest of the application that they are going to be unable to get out from under it. That doesn't necessarily mean that if you are a quiet person, you should avoid the interview, because there are quiet people who do very well in business school and in business. The truth is, by the time people come to interview with us, by and large, they have been through many interviews before and are reasonably comfortable in that situation. For those who are not, I think that if they can get past the first five minutes, they're fine.

Melinda   To be honest, I wouldn't counsel anyone to avoid the interview. To me, you have to take the personality issue out of the interview. Most of us tend to gravitate toward people who are more similar to us. That doesn't mean, however, that the person who is different is not going to add value in the classroom.

I think that most people tend to assume automatically that more outgoing, extroverted people will tend to do better in interviews. Maybe they do; but there are some people who are very outgoing who never give you anything of substance, whereas more introverted, contemplative people will give you more substantial answers. I think you have to be careful in assuming that a particular type of personality makes for a better interview.

Michael   Some applicants are excellent writers, have good GPAs, and have done well on the GMAT; but their maturity level might not be that high or they may not communicate ideas well person-to-person. We might not catch this outside an interview; so, in some cases, the interview is an advantage for the school.

Then you have applicants who maybe didn't get the 3.8 GPA as an undergrad, who didn't get the 700 on the GMAT, but they've done some good things. They've had jobs in which they've had to be effective communicators and in which they've played significant roles in teams. They've really made an impact at work, and it shows. Those things come across in an interview where they might not on paper. For people who match this profile, the interview can provide an advantage.

Jeremy   If you are someone who is self-assured in his delivery and tends to be confident in one-to-one situations, rather than being the high stress type, then you'll perform well in the interview. Interviews are also really helpful in situations where the interviewer has something to offer that is unique. While people will describe these aspects of their lives in the written application, I find that often it doesn't jump out at you in the same way as when the individual is there to put some emotion and context behind it. If you have someone, for instance, who has done something entrepreneurial, or has traveled in Africa for a couple of years, or has done an enormous amount of person-to-person community work, I want to hear about these experiences, as they help me to get a good sense of somebody. They don't have to have had the best grades, graduated from an Ivy League college, or worked for a blue-chip investment bank to be appealing to a business school admissions committee.

Mark I think people who are outgoing—but not flagrantly aggressive—are good interview candidates. I know of at least one candidate who was so overwhelmingly obnoxious in the interview that the interviewer wrote, "I don't care what this person's credentials are; do not let him in." Therefore, if you're a little bit overwhelming in person, you might avoid interviewing. In addition, if you look very good on paper, but get excessively nervous during interviews, I'd probably pass on the interview.

I think people who have really thought through their application perform best. If you have to rush an application, I wouldn't interview.

Martin I don't think I would counsel almost anyone to avoid the interview. I think that the interview gives the applicant the time to ask questions. There is a lot of give and take; and if the candidate is interviewing with a student, he sees at least one representative of the student body.

If you are really nervous in those types of situations, you may want to pass. In addition, if you're absolutely confident in your application, then maybe there is no point in interviewing if it is just going to be icing on the cake. People in that situation, in fact, might also want to avoid the interview because they might have the remote chance of ruining something that is already a "sure thing."

4. What are your top three favorite questions to ask in an interview?

Henry One of my top questions is, "How did you choose the particular college that you attended?" I think this allows us not only to hear something about who the applicant was at 18, but also a bit about what her thought process is in choosing an institution. Perhaps we can use that information later on; for example, if a person said, "I chose UCLA because I wanted a really big program," and she comes back to you later and says, "Now I want a really small program," you can then push her on that issue and ask, "Why do you think that? You chose a big school before."

The natural bias of an admissions officer is, "I want all of my students to be from a name-brand school." In reality, people often select a school because of financial, geographical, and family reasons. When you hear that someone picked one school over another because of family or peer pressure, because everyone in the family went to that school, or because he couldn't afford to go to a particular school, this gives you some sense of his values. In addition, if a person says to me, "I was admitted to Ivy League schools One, Two, and Three and chose to go to No Name School Four instead," unless I am a complete cynic and refuse to believe he got into Harvard, Princeton, and Yale, that tells me something about his intellect right there.

Another question I often use is, "If you were coming back for your fifth reunion, what would you like people to remember about you from your days as a student here?" In contrast, I'm not a big fan of the question, "What are you going to be doing ten years from now?" To be honest, nobody really knows. A variation on this theme: "Let's now pretend that we're at graduation. Tell me the award you would most like to be presented."

My other favorite question is "Is there anything that we haven't asked you that you would like to be asked?" That is the applicant's opportunity to explain, for example, why he got a 320 GMAT. For me, it is essential to ask this question. After you've heard 45 minutes of self-congratulation, you may now find out about a weakness or two.

Melinda   I don't have three specific ones. We ask about things that we care about in a Fuqua student, such as teamwork skills, honesty and integrity, enthusiasm, goals, and level of initiative. We also care about differences, unique experiences, backgrounds, and perceptions. We ask questions that will specifically target things like leadership potential, teamwork skills, goals, ethics, and flexibility. We tend to favor a moderately scheduled interview that will enable us to explore these issues.

With leadership, for example, I ask people about their best learning experiences, either at school or at work, or an opportunity they have had to lead a group. This line of inquiry tends to get at both leadership skills and teamwork skills.

Michael   I really try to vary it. I have an informal list of roughly 30 questions. I don't have anything specific that I ask all the time.

My interviews are probably longer than the average, about one to one and a half hours. The first hour, we're talking about them. I want to give candidates the chance to show their stuff. A lot of times, people are nervous, and things don't come across all that well in the beginning. I want to give them a chance to settle down. In the other 30 minutes, most candidates usually have a pretty fair number of questions, and I spend time answering those.

Before I went to Kellogg, I spent some time talking to one of their alums, which really helped me solidify the fact that I wanted to go there. I was grateful for his time. He told me some good things about the school and gave me some "insider pointers" of what the school is like, and I really appreciated that. I had a good experience at Kellogg, and for me, interviewing as an alum is a way to give something back to the program.

Jeremy   I generally ask one about a candidate's community work. "Tell me about your work with the Juvenile Diabetes Foundation," I might ask. A lot of applicants have not spent meaningful amounts of time doing that sort of thing. When asked about their community work, some people who have been less involved exhibit a kind of mature acceptance and will tell you right up front, "Well, I haven't really done a lot of that." Others, however, will get defensive and founder. "Oh my God," they think, "is this some sort of fatal flaw that will be held against me?" It's not, but it is interesting to see how they react to a question about an area to which they may not have devoted a lot of time.

Another that I use is, "Tell me what leadership means to you and ways in which you have manifested your leadership skills in the past." When somebody has a crystalline understanding of what leadership means to them and can lay out for you what she's done under that model of leadership, it can be a powerful statement in her favor.

Mark   As an applicant, the question that you just have to be able to answer is: Why this business school? The key is not only to have a coherent answer about why your background leads you to wanting or needing an MBA, but also being able to differentiate between the school you're interviewing with and other schools. For example, if you're interviewing with Chicago and Kellogg and you can't make a dramatic differentiation between the two schools, it will hurt you. The schools are utterly different. If you can't convey to people that you understand that and that one school fits you better than the other, that's probably trouble.

Another one that I like is: "If you had to choose between going to a party Friday night and doing some extra studying for a Monday morning midterm, what would you do?" A question like that will help you to find out if the person is so uptight that she can't give you an honest answer or that she's willing to sacrifice the social side of business school to squeeze out a better grade. As much as you want people who are going to be strong contributors in the classroom, you also need people who are going to be good representatives of the school once they're done. People who would pass on the party worry me.

Martin Some of the questions I like include: "What would you like to be known for when you die? What would you like your epitaph to read?" "What would you like people to say about you at your retirement party?" "Tell me something unusual about yourself," and "What do you add to a group when you take on a team assignment or group task?"

5. What is the most difficult or unusual question you've ever put to a prospective student?

Henry When somebody volunteers a negative piece of information, the follow-up question to that can be difficult. If somebody says, "I didn't do very well in college and got a 2.3 GPA," you need to then decide if you want to ask the question "How did that happen?" It may be opening a can of worms. When you're probing at negative issues, that's always difficult for the applicant because obviously the applicant would like you to come away feeling 100 percent positive about him.

We don't ask questions like "What vegetable would you be?" I think those are really odd questions. They just don't get any valuable information. You end up thinking, "Well, that's kind of a weird answer." I feel like I ask fairly predictable, straightforward questions. In most cases, what you are doing is asking a question to let a person talk. "Tell me the vegetable" just doesn't do it, because then there you are with the answer, "Tomato," and what do you do with that?

I had a colleague who used to ask the question, "If you could relive one day in your life, which one would it be?" That makes you think, "What do I say? Do I say 'The day I helped Mother Theresa'? Do I say 'The day that I got into college'? Do I say 'The day that I got this job'?" It's a good question on one level, but the problem with a question like that is that immediately the applicant thinks, "How does the interviewer want me to answer this question?" It's like asking an applicant "Who did you vote for in the last presidential election?" They're looking at you thinking, "He's in education, so he's probably a Democrat. But he works for a business school, so he might be a Republican."

Melinda Sometimes people have to think hard about different questions. I've talked to people who had a difficult time coming up with an ethical dilemma, for example. I've interviewed applicants who have had a hard time defining their most significant personal achievements. It really depends on the person as to what question is more difficult for her.

My attitude in a business school interview is, "This is not an opportunity for us to grill someone." You can get what you want from somebody and do it pleasantly. I want to get to know what a person can contribute to this academic community. My questions don't tend or need to be particularly hard-nosed.

Michael A lot of people go to Kellogg because of its strength in marketing. If an applicant expresses this kind of interest, I will ask him to give me an example of an ad he's seen recently and to tell me why it's good or where it falls short. The applicants I interview are frequently not from the advertising world. They're coming from an engineering background, a banking background, or the like. But if they want to go into marketing, part of the assumption is that they are interested in related issues and have some opinions. They don't need to answer the same way that I would—I'm just looking for their thought process and to see if they can think on their feet.

Jeremy I have a natural cynicism towards applicants who have participated in the standard two-year analyst program. When I interview someone with that sort of profile, I ask, "In the sea of two-year analysts we are seeing this year in the application process, what do you think makes you different? What do you think that you would provide to our school community that would be something special?" I think that a lot of people in that situation have never stopped to think about the potentially undifferentiated position that they are in. They've been thinking, "Well, I've got this strong GMAT, went to a great school, have been working at Salomon Brothers for two years, and have some good recommendations. This is going to be a breeze. So-and-so from the firm got in last year, and this is what a lot of MBAs look like." You get a funny reaction when they suddenly realize what you're getting at. It's a challenge to them to think about how they are truly different.

Mark I think that questions regarding specific elements of an applicant's background can be tough. If the candidate had, say, a particularly difficult year in school, it's the kind of thing that he will most likely bury and try to avoid in an interview, particularly if he was having personal problems. I think that questions that reveal skeletons in the closet make people squirm. Some applicants have thought through their past well and can give you good answers, while other people don't really respond.

Martin I don't think that any of the general questions are tough or awkward. It's usually the specific and pointed questions about things that they have on their resumes that can be difficult; for if something doesn't look quite kosher, I'll ask about it. These probing questions are sometimes painful to answer; for example, one person I spoke with had his GMAT scores on his resume. They were really low, so I didn't understand why he was exposing them to the world. I almost assumed they were on there for a reason and that he expected to be asked about them because he had done so poorly. So I asked, "Why do you think that your GMAT scores are so low?" The person flushed and stuttered; it was an embarrassing moment for him. I still never determined why that information was on the resume.

6. How do you think an applicant can best prepare for an interview?

Henry Take a really hard look at your resume. Go back and start with college and be ready to talk about any piece of who you've been since the age of 17 or 18. Be willing to talk about the successes and failures you've had along the way.

In addition, you should be prepared to talk about why you want the degree. In our case, we are asking students to make a two-year, $75,000 commitment. Obviously, we don't hold people to what they say they're going to do two years later; but it sure makes it easier to admit someone who has an idea of where he might head, rather than a person who simply says "It just seems like the right thing to do right now" or "My dad wants me to do this." I think it is also fair to say that most applicants haven't planned all the details of their futures. But when a person comes in and says, "I want to go into consulting," he needs an answer when I ask him what kind of consulting. If he can't respond to the second question, then he hasn't thought things through very well. I try to ask a candidate to link the MBA with what he's done before and what he might then do in the future. If you can present a clear rationale for how those three are going to fit together, then you've done the homework you need to do before the interview.

You should also have a thorough knowledge of the school at which you are interviewing. If you make sweeping statements in the interview like, "I'm only applying to small general management programs" and then say "And I'm applying to Harvard and Tuck," this makes you look ill-informed, for while they are both general management programs, one is not small.

Melinda   Knowing what you want and knowing why business school would be a good step at this point in your career, knowing the kind of program you are looking for, and doing your research about the school are all essential. If you do these things, then you'll do well in an interview.

Michael   A candidate should have a clear idea of what he wants to do and why. If you're going to go back to a full-time MBA program like a Northwestern or a Harvard or a Wharton and will spend $20 to $30 thousand a year to do so, you should know where you're headed and how the MBA helps you to get there. Do a little bit of soul searching before you apply.

I go back to my undergraduate institution and talk to students there about getting into MBA programs. When they ask me about what they need to do and say, I tell them that they need to be honest. You're not going to know everything about your future direction when you apply. You're not necessarily going to be able to say, "I want to be an account executive for Leo Burnett." But, if you want to go into advertising, you should have some reasons why beyond "I've always been interested in ads and like the ones I see on TV." Having talked to people in the industry and having done informational interviews tells me that at least the applicant has an idea of what the job is like and why he wants to pursue it.

In addition, be ready to ask deep, penetrating questions. When an applicant does so, this tells me not only that he has thought about what he wants to do, but also that he's done his homework on the program. There is a difference between someone who tells me, at the end of the interview, "Well, I don't have any real questions," versus someone who says, "Can you tell me why Kellogg's curriculum allows you to take as many concentrations as you want? Doesn't that make you a jack of all trades?" People who are savvy understand that the interview isn't over when I tell them that it is their turn to ask questions.

Jeremy   You need to understand why you want to go to business school at all and what you hope the experience will mean to you. Are you just interested in buying yourself a valuable option for future opportunities, or is there something specific about the experience that intrigues you?

You also need to understand what is potentially unique or interesting about your background and express this well in the interview. There may be thousands of applicants applying to the same school to which you are applying. You're just another face. I think the typical on-campus interviewer might talk to 200 to 250 students in a year. An alum might see as few as four or as many as 50 or more. If you can differentiate yourself well, you can avoid being lost in the numbing wash of applications and interviews that admissions committee members face. To do this effectively is a staggering challenge.

I have a few individuals who just jump out at me in my memory. For example, there was one guy who was a platoon commander in the navy SEALS who just dripped leadership. I left that interview sweating, thinking, "This guy is unbelievable." Another example that comes to mind was an African American woman whom I interviewed who came absolutely out of nowhere. She didn't graduate initially from high school, worked as a maid and a waitress, graduated on her own from high school at 20-something, fought her way through a bachelor's degree somewhere, then got hired by this visionary guy. She rose through this man's company quickly and eventually applied to Wharton.

Maybe these examples are too extreme for the average applicant to relate to, but I think the reality is that the individual thinks that he is quite special; and, in the context of his family, work, and friends, he probably is. But there are a lot of good people against whom you'll be competing in the application process, and you need to set yourself apart.

Mark   First, know your own application well. In large part, interviewers will ask a lot of the same kind of questions you get on the application to cross-check the validity of the answers and how comfortable you are giving them. If you are applying to multiple schools, I think that you also need to have a good explanation for what interests you about each program.

I also advise applicants to practice in interview situations so that they're as comfortable as possible. If you have a reasonably social personality, you want that to come through; and if there are any rough edges or any doubts that show up on paper, you might be able to smooth those over a bit if you can interview well. To prepare yourself for an interview, call people who are at the school if you know them; talk to them about your application and about the way they might evaluate it. Current students alert you to any hot buttons that the school has, which will enable you to make sure that you don't say something that is going to offend an administrator. Talking to the people at the school is invaluable. You can really tell the difference in an interview between people who are strictly getting brochures, looking through them, and then applying and applicants who know people who have gone to the school and have talked to them.

Martin   I had one applicant who even did research on me. It was too funny. He came in and said, "Well, I know you've gone to law school and that you're originally from Texas." I was floored. Piqued, too. That was overdoing it a bit.

I think you have to know a lot about the program, because clearly, you're going to get the question about why you might want to go to a particular business school. You also have to be prepared to talk about anything on your resume. Anything at all. If you're not, then it has no business being on your resume. In addition, you should know something about the geographic region in which the school is located; for example, with Columbia, you should know a bit about metropolitan New York.

Finally, be prepared to ask questions that may be a little out of the ordinary. In the interview, you are likely to develop a rapport with the interviewer that will make you more comfortable asking tough or odd questions. If this happens, go ahead and ask the questions that you always wondered about but were afraid to ask.

7. Do you think that an applicant will gain any competitive advantage by interviewing on campus versus interviewing off campus with an alumnus or other university representative?

Henry   The advantage of the on-campus interview is that you have a chance to see the school in action before the interview session. This means, if you're smart, you can incorporate what you've seen that day into some of your answers. However, the admissions officers at Tuck actually interview three times as many people off campus as on. We go to 18 cities domestically and another five abroad; it's part of our recruitment strategy. Our hope is that the off-campus interview might then spark a visit or that a visit has sparked the off-campus interview. I would say that people who have been on campus and then interview off campus are at an advantage, because, as mentioned earlier, they may be better prepared for the interview. But we weigh the two kinds of interviews the same.

Melinda   We only interview on campus; and, in a lot of ways, that is a competitive advantage for us. Applicants often cite their visit here as being a very positive experience. Candidates are able to have lunch with current students, sit in on classes, tour the campus, etc.

Michael   That's hard for me to say, as I've never been part of the on-campus interviewing process. When I applied to Kellogg, for example, I also interviewed off campus. The one advantage I see to the on-campus option is that you get to see the school, meet the people, and get a flavor for what the school is like. The flip side, however, is that admissions staff members are probably doing two or three interviews that day, whereas an alum might only conduct four or five interviews a season. I've done up to nine in a season, but I'll do one every two or three weeks. As a result, I may have more time to concentrate on the candidate.

Jeremy   People like me do not face as many applicants. I see a small enough number that I can devote a lot of thought and creativity to writing up a report on each individual, so there may be some benefit there.

On the other hand, I would recommend that individuals go to campus anyway because you cannot help but to benefit from visiting the school and seeing what it's like. I don't know how many people I've interviewed who have told me, after having had a chance to attend classes and spend time on campus, that Wharton is not at all as they imagined it to be. The environment is totally different and far more enjoyable and relaxed than they ever could have expected.

If you do go on campus and have your eyes open, it could be a big opportunity for you to express your insights to the interviewer about what you've seen. This can give the interviewer a very positive impression about a candidate.

Mark   I think that if you present yourself well in interview situations, you probably should go ahead and interview on campus. An on-campus interviewer is very possibly involved in other aspects of the interview process, and, if you make a good impression, it may carry extra weight. In contrast, if you interview with an alumnus, he is not as likely to be involved elsewhere in the decision-making process, so his weight may be confined to the interview evaluation.

Martin   No, I don't think there is an advantage to interviewing on campus. I think that the interview is generally a stressful situation. If you are out of the business school setting and with an alumnus or a student who may not be dressed to the hilt, you will probably relax more. I would also think that because the students and the alumni are not professional interviewers, we might be more lax than the admissions staff.

On the other hand, students and alumni have not interviewed as many applicants as have the members of the admissions staff. The advantage of meeting with people from the admissions office is that they know what the entire range of applicants look like. They know how and whether you would fit into the entering class.

8. If your school uses a mix of admissions committee members and current students to conduct on-campus interviews, can an applicant voice a preference as to with whom he would like to interview? Does it matter?

Henry   It does not matter. The applicant can voice a preference, but there are no guarantees because we are out of the office so much. In effect, if you come on campus, you are probably going to interview with a student. Sometimes people do express a preference, and to the extent that we can accommodate them, we will. But the reality is that schedules change. We tell candidates in the interview-confirmation letter that "You'll be interviewing with a member of the admissions committee," which is true. If we know that interviewer is also going to be a student, we will tell them that, too. However, in the letter, we do not say that you will definitely be interviewing with an admissions officer, because someone can suddenly need to go out of town, and then we're faced with an applicant who is angry with us. People believe that it is better to interview with one of us. I think, however, that this is not necessarily true. We take the interview write-up produced by a student just as seriously as we do one that was written by a member of the staff.

It is worth noting that student interviewers, regardless of institution, have probably an even higher vested interest in who gets in than do the admissions officers, as they are protecting their investment in the degree. As a result, sometimes interviews with students can be tough.

Melinda An applicant can always voice a preference, but that does not mean that one of those people will be available. We schedule interviews on a first-come, first-served basis. An applicant can say, "I really want to interview with the director of admissions," but if the director already has a full schedule, then there is not much we can do about it. It really does not matter because our students who are on the admissions committee have a vote equal to mine in admissions committee meetings. The person who has read the file comes to the meeting and talks about everything that is covered in the application; the person who interviewed the applicant talks about the interview, and together, we make a decision.

Michael Not to my knowledge. It's pretty much a blind process.

Jeremy As far as I know, they do not have a direct way of voicing such a preference. At Wharton, there is a schedule, and the administration will just pencil your name in when you make your request.

Mark I don't think you can voice a preference. I suppose if you scheduled an interview and found out you would be speaking with someone with whom you would prefer not to meet, you could attempt to reschedule the interview and hope for a change. This could be tricky, however.

Whether you are better or worse off interviewing with a student depends on how well-prepared you are. If you are well-prepared and you are comfortable with yourself, you will do fine with either an administrator or a student. If you are not ready for the interview, you actually may fare better with an administrator. A student is likely to start off being friendly, very willing to give you a chance. However, if you don't answer basic questions about your application well, or if you can't tell him, for example, why your grades might have slipped one quarter or why you took a year off from work, he may become more and more difficult. If you're really bad, he may bury you. I don't think an administrator will ever do that. He will most likely be polite regardless, while the student may very well punish you.

If you do end up talking to an administrator, try to be calm. If your interviewer is a student, you can be a little more nervous and he's going to be understanding. He's also going to give you less of the party line; he'll be a lot more relaxed about the whole story that the administration may be trying to pitch. You can be less formal with a student, whereas I think that you should maintain a higher degree of formality with an administrator.

Martin   Columbia is vague in that it has two admissions periods, September and January, and a lot depends on the time of year. During the early fall, we have an open-door policy, and interviews are generally conducted in-house with a student or an administrator. Normally, an applicant can't choose the interviewer, and I don't think it makes a difference.

9. What irritates you most during an interview?

Henry   Having people cut me off. Not listening to the question. Those are the biggies.

Melinda   People who I think are trying to come up with the "right" answer, who are too intent on making a good impression or anticipating what they think that I want to hear to be able to just give me themselves. I want the person; that's all I want. When people are not confident enough to be themselves, it does bother me.

Michael   When candidates don't listen to the entire question and respond before I'm finished. If they answer immediately after I'm finished, that tells me either that they are not listening or that they have a canned response. You usually can tell.

Jeremy   One trivial thing that both amuses and irritates me is when somebody gets the name of the school wrong. Once I can understand, twice is unforgivable. To me, it implies that the applicant does not really have a profound interest in attending that school, that he was just completing the application to better his statistical chances of getting in somewhere.

More profound irritation comes when I get a sense that the applicant has not thought through why he is applying. Coming in with a low sense of self-awareness is a kiss of death. Candidates should go take a weekend retreat, bring a piece of paper, and think through these things. Challenge yourself to understand why you want to do this.

Arrogance is another good way to get yourself knocked out immediately.

Mark   Lack of preparedness and arrogance run neck and neck as far as ways to get yourself dinged. If you're arrogant, if you come across as demanding "What can your school do for me?" you won't get in. If you come across as not knowing anything about the school, if you don't understand, for example, that Chicago is a good finance school or that Kellogg is a good marketing school or that Harvard does primarily case method versus lecture, there's a problem. Those are pretty fundamental things, and if you're not aware of these facts, the interviewer is going to wonder why you're even applying. Finally, know your own background. If someone asks you about your grades or your work experience and you can't answer some straight-forward questions, he will wonder whether you're being truthful, and that will get you in trouble in a hurry.

Martin   Dishonesty. People who just spout platitudes.

For additional advice on interviewing, we've included information on several popular books on the subject. While we have not prepared for interviews ourselves using these books, the content looked good upon review. Although these books are geared for job hunters, they contain information that will be useful for business school applicants as well.

Power Interviews: Job Winning Tactics from Fortune 500 Recruiters, Neil Yeager and Lee Hough, John Wiley & Sons, Inc.

Smart Questions: Interview Your Way to Job Success, Dorothy Leeds, HarperPaperbacks

The Perfect Interview: How to Get the Job You Really Want, John D. Drake, Amacom

The Smart Woman's Guide to Interviewing and Salary Negotiation, Julie Adair King, Career Press

10

Packaging the Product

Clothes make the man. Naked people have little or no influence in society.

MARK TWAIN
Attributed

Despite your best efforts to crafting thoughtful, articulate essays, if you package your final product poorly, you will dilute its impact on your intended audience. Application readers review hundreds of completed applications each fall. Sending them incomplete data sheets and illegible handwritten essays doesn't make their job any easier and certainly doesn't cast a good light on you as a candidate.

We've covered some of the initial steps of the production and packaging of your application in Chapter 2. Again, it's essential that you tackle some of the logistics issues early on. When your application packet finally arrives in the mail, rip it open, dump the contents on the rug, and sort through the various components so that you know what needs to be done when. Once you've sent in your transcript request forms and mailed the appropriate materials to your recommenders, move on to the innumerable data sheets and information cards. This material gives the schools a summary of key background data that they will need to process your application: mailing address, phone number, undergraduate institution attended, past employers, and the like. Although typewriters seem to be following the evolutionary path of the Triceratops and the passenger pigeon, it's probably a good idea to dig up a typewriter to complete these forms unless your handwriting is excellent. As Phil's looks like Sumerian cuneiform on a bad day, this was essential. He borrowed a Brother electric typewriter from a friend. If you don't own a typewriter or can't find a friend who does, you can frequently rent one to use on-site for a modest cost at copy shops such as Kinko's.

PACKAGING YOUR ESSAYS

To complete the application essays themselves, use either a typewriter or, better yet, a computer and a laser printer. (A number of MBA programs now offer their applications on a diskette. If this option is available to you, you may well want to take it. It's certainly convenient.) In our opinion, having access to a computer with decent word processing software and a high quality printer is a must for the MBA application process, especially if you are planning to complete multiple applications. The ability to edit your work quickly and easily is essential. Given the amount of overlap in the subject matter of different schools' application essays, you'll find that a word processor's "cut and paste" functions are a godsend.

In completing both the essays and the informational forms, stick with a reasonable font size: We recommend either 10 or 12 point. Application readers simply won't have the time or patience to read material in a type that is much smaller: Make their jobs easier and they'll be thankful to you. If an application form explicitly requests you to use at least 12-point fonts, follow this guideline. In addition, leave yourself reasonable margins to allow readers to make notes on your essays. If you find yourself leaving one-eighth-inch margins and using 8 point Times Roman in your essays, you're trying to say too much. Get back to the word processor and do some rigorous editing. When you've trimmed your essays down to a more sensible length, print them and see how they look. You'll often catch errors reading a printed copy that you missed when gazing at the computer screen. Some applications have no specific forms on which you are to print your essays. For those that do, make photocopies of these forms so that you can test the alignment of your essays when you run them through the printer. When you've waited for weeks to receive critical application forms, the last thing you want to do is muck up your originals when you're up against a tight deadline.

INCLUDING SUPPLEMENTARY MATERIALS

One question many candidates face is whether or not to include supplementary materials in their application packages. We asked Linda Baldwin, the Director of Admissions for UCLA's Andersen School of Business (from whom you'll hear more in Chapter 12):

"If a student sends you additional material, will you read it, and what is the upper boundary when it comes to extras?" She answered, "We usually don't need poems, videos, or tapes of you singing, although I've been sent such things on occasion. The photos are OK, but some of them can get a bit redundant—I've received family albums. I would say that three recommendations would be fine, four would be top level—you probably don't need more than four. You don't need annual reports from your companies and things like that (a lot of people don't think we know where they worked). There really isn't a need to send your undergraduate honors thesis either. Keep it short. Send in your application. Spend more of your time answering the questions."

So while there are no clear-cut guidelines as to what supplementary materials an applicant may send, our recommendation is to use common sense. You know that application readers don't have a wealth of time to spend with each application, so don't send them a copy of the 545-page textbook you wrote on the life of the earthworm. It's also not a good idea to send something of value that you want returned to you. If you include additional information, make it something that complements your essays and that can be reviewed relatively quickly. You might send a picture or two of a product or project on which you worked, with a brief verbal explanation, as we saw in Chapter 8. When Phil submitted his applications, he enclosed a copy of an article he had written for a managerial journal. One of Phil's essays described his interest in writing as a key extracurricular interest. A final note on this issue: At a handful of schools, such as Harvard, the GMAT is no longer required or even accepted as part of the admissions process. The admissions committee really means it when they say they don't want this information. No matter how well you do, refrain from submitting this data. Sending in your score will not win you brownie points; rather, admissions officers will view this as an annoyance.

SUBMITTING AN UNFINISHED APPLICATION

Another common question that applicants have is whether they should submit an application that is "almost complete" in order to meet an impending deadline. The short answer to this question is "No." Even if all you are missing is one of your three recommendations or a single essay question, admissions committees will not review your application until it is 100 percent complete. If your application is missing various elements, the admissions staff will wait until you deliver the rest of the material and will evaluate it during the next admissions period that season.

MANAGING QUALITY CONTROL

Once you do have all the pieces of your application together, the next step is to engage in quality control. Most of your applications will come with a checklist that details the various components that should be included in a completed application. Go through this checklist and make sure that you've completed all of the material they require. This is especially important when you're completing multiple applications. It's easy to forget to include something when you've got piles of forms and essays on your desk from five or six schools. Forgetting to enclose an important form or other piece of material can slow down the application review process. In addition, make sure you return the right forms to the appropriate schools. Sending your Columbia data sheet to the University of Michigan would be an embarrassing faux pas.

When your application is completed, make a photocopy of it for your files. After all this work, you should make sure you don't have to start from scratch should your application get swallowed up in a Postal Service void. Regardless of how you choose to submit your application, you should definitely complete and include the self-addressed postcard in the application packet. This card will be returned to you once the admissions office has received your package. If this postcard doesn't materialize within a few weeks of mailing your application, call and investigate. Applications do get lost, and pieces of your application can easily slide off the mail table.

To decrease the odds of your application disappearing into a black hole, consider mailing your application one of two ways. First, you can send it registered mail, return receipt requested. It won't get there any faster, but at least you'll have another way of knowing that someone on the other end received it. You'll also know when your application was received. Another recommended delivery mechanism is the Postal Service's Priority Mail pack. Your application gets there quickly and at a reasonable cost. The downside of this approach, however, is that there is no tracking number assigned to the package, and you do not receive a receipt that indicates the package arrived at its destination. For those who are desperate for time, use an overnight delivery service, such as Federal Express (FedEx), Airborne Express, UPS, or Express Mail.

They'll assign a tracking number to your package so you'll be able to verify that it arrived. Sending your applications via overnight delivery is an expensive habit, however. What's more, the dramatic arrival of your package is witnessed only by the mailroom staff. Once there, it is stripped of its colorful, costly overnight packaging and put into a pile with all the rest of the applications. The applications readers never know of the effort and expense you went to to rush your materials to them this way.

11

The Envelope, Please

If at first you don't succeed, you are running about average.

M.H. ALDERSON
Reader's Digest, February 1976

THE WAIT

Waiting for a decision from your target schools may be the most difficult part of the application process. You've done everything within your power to influence their decision, and you're then stuck cooling your heels for weeks or even months while you wait for them to get back to you. It's hard to be patient during this period, but worrying about the outcome isn't going to do any good. So our advice is that you plunge back into other activities to take your mind off waiting.

You probably have not seen as much of your friends as you'd have liked to in the last several weeks, so go out and have some fun. If you have a significant other, he or she will be glad to tear you away from your word processor and will appreciate your attention. You may have let work slide a bit. Dive into your professional life again and try to learn whatever else you can in your current job, for you may be leaving it behind in a couple of months.

When you do finally hear from the schools to which you applied, the news will come in one of four forms: admit, deny, waitlist, or deferral. This chapter will discuss each form.

ADMIT

If a school grants you admission to its MBA program, it will either notify you by mail or by phone. Phone calls are followed up by a formal letter (it's always nice to have something tangible!). When we applied, we received phone calls from a handful of schools, including Dartmouth's Tuck School and UCLA. The phone calls are a nice personal touch and, in our opinion, a good marketing effort on behalf of those schools that invest in the time to make them. A word to the wise: If you don't want the whole office to know of your good fortune, make sure you note on your application that you would like to receive phone calls at home. Receiving these calls from an enthusiastic admissions director can be a bit awkward if you're trying to keep the news of your imminent departure a closely held secret at work.

If you do receive a phone call, you may well end up trading voicemail messages with someone for a while before you actually reach a live person. Try not to prejudge the message. It took Carol three days to reach someone at Tuck after having received a message from an admissions officer. She was in agony during the waiting period. "Did the director sound cheerful on the phone," she wondered, "or is this bad news?" You're not going to get an offer of admission via voicemail, and you're certainly not going to be able to decode the admissions officer's intentions by listening for voice intonation. So just relax; you'll figure things out soon enough.

Remember that receiving a phone call doesn't always mean that the admissions office has made a decision. Carol was ecstatic when she got a message from UCLA on our answering machine at home. When she called them back, she was disappointed to learn that they were simply missing a piece of paperwork and that they had called to make sure she got it to them as soon as possible.

Eventually, however, your schools of choice will get around to making a decision. Whether or not you hear the news by phone, you will certainly get written notification of your offer for admission. Don't be disappointed if you find a thin envelope awaiting you in the mailbox one day after work. Some schools, such as Harvard, send you a preliminary notification first and wait a week or two before deluging you with supplementary materials.

An admissions letter will read something like the one that follows. Please note that all letters in this chapter have been modeled after actual documents exchanged between applicants and representatives of the country's top business schools. Copyright law kept us from using the originals. The names of all schools and admissions directors have been changed, but the spirit and much of the wording of these letters are consistent with their sources.

Dear Ms. Keating:

It is a pleasure to offer you admission to the Master of Business Administration Program at the Western Graduate School of Business. We are certain that you will make the most of Western's opportunities for intellectual and personal growth and know that you have much to contribute to the Business School community. We sincerely hope that you will choose to pursue your management education here at Western.

We are holding an open house for admitted students on April 15 to give you the chance to speak with current students and future classmates, as well as to meet faculty and members of the administration. Further information about the open house will be sent to you under separate cover in the near future. In addition, you will also receive a phone call from a current student to answer any questions you may have about life at the WSB.

In the meantime, please read the information on financial aid that we have included for your review. Should you have any questions about loans or fellowships, feel free to call the Financial Aid Office at 415-555-3197.

Please note that your admission is for the fall. To secure your space in the class, we must receive the Admitted Student Reply Card and the WSB-MBA Admissions Information Sheet by May 2.

Please let us know if we can provide you with any information that may help you with your decision. Our enthusiasm to have you enroll here at Western not only reflects our assessment of your past achievements, but also our faith in your future abilities and contributions. We hope to see you here in October.

Best regards,

Marcia Covey
Director of Admissions

Schools will give you several weeks to several months to make a decision, depending on when you applied. Don't be hasty. This is clearly an important choice. We'll talk about the decision-making process later in the chapter, but for now, hang tight and wait until you know what all of your options are before you send in that postcard. And, by the way, congratulations!

DENY

If an MBA program decides to deny your application for admission, it is unlikely that the admissions staff is going to let you know over the phone. Instead, you'll receive a letter that looks something like this one:

Dear John:

After careful consideration, the Committee on Admissions regrets that it cannot act favorably on your application for admission to the Eastern School of Business Administration MBA program.

We are able to admit only a small number of those who apply to our program and must make difficult choices in allocating the available spaces. We anticipate more than 2,000 applications this year for an entering class of less than 240 students. The fact that we have not offered you admission should not be taken as a reflection of your intellectual abilities, personal achievement, or potential for success in management. Your application received a thorough review by a group comprised of members from the Committee on Admissions. In most cases, there is no single reason for a decision not to offer an applicant admission.

I regret that we are unable to respond to telephone inquiries concerning the decision on your application. Any questions concerning the Committee's decision should be put in writing and will receive a response after our application process has been completed in early July.

Thank you for your interest in Eastern School. I wish you success in pursuing graduate management study and in your future career.

Sincerely,

Alfred Cespedes
Director of Admissions

If a letter like this darkens your doorstep, try not to be too discouraged. If you've taken the advice in this book to heart, you've applied to a portfolio of different schools to spread your risk. Being rejected from one program, then, should not mean that you're trapped in your current job for another year. The odds are that one of your other bets will pan out. If for some reason, however, you do have your heart set on one particular institution, don't jump off any bridges quite yet. MBA programs are generally more than willing to consider an application again the following year. In fact, if you chose to, you could submit the exact same application once more the next fall. Most programs will keep your applications on file for at least two years after you have applied, so conceivably, you would not even have to send them the materials again the next year.

If you do plan to reapply to a particular program, however, our advice is to modify your application somewhat for the next round. With another year of work experience, you clearly have more material from which to draw in writing your essays. Maybe you've accomplished something extraordinary in your professional life that is worth including in your "most substantial accomplishments" essay. Perhaps you've become involved in a community service program and want to share stories of your experiences as a volunteer as part of your "extracurricular interests" essay. You also might want to include a new letter of recommendation. Admissions committee members want to see how you've grown both as a professional and as an individual since you last applied. Improving on your original application gives you the chance to show them what you've learned in the meantime and to communicate how the experiences you've had in the interim period make you a more effective candidate.

To understand exactly why you were rejected and to identify the areas on which you may need to work, swallow your pride and ask. The admissions office at most business schools will be glad to give you written or verbal commentary as to why you were not accepted and how you can strengthen your candidacy in the future. In any case, don't let this criticism deflate your ego. Rather, consider it to be inside information, valuable insight into the thinking of your target audience that can help you to adjust your personal positioning for the next application season. Once you understand what the admissions committee considered to be your shortcomings, you can work to strengthen those areas, and, as a result, you will be able to market yourself more effectively.

Were you told that you didn't have enough quantitative training? Take a course or two in economics, calculus, or statistics at night at a local community college. (An aside: For those with rusty quantitative skills, many schools have math refresher courses during the week or so before school starts. Enrolling in a formal course beforehand, however, both shows additional commitment and gives you more practice in areas you may find problematic.) Were you criticized for not having had much leadership experience? Lobby for the opportunity to lead a project at work, or join a community service effort in which you can take a leadership role.

Persistence can pay off. A friend of ours applied three times to Harvard's MBA program before she was accepted. She ended up being one of the most conscientious students we met during our two years in Cambridge. We felt that, as a result of her arduous acceptance process, she got more out of the experience than other, younger students who got in straight away and treated school like a two-year vacation. Scott McNealy, the president and founder of Sun Microsystems, applied to Stanford at least three times before he was accepted. The admissions process can be an imperfect one. If you are interested enough in a particular program to defer returning to school for another shot at that institution, find out where you fall short and take action to shore up those supposed weak spots.

WAITLIST

Being waitlisted by a school you care about can be an extremely frustrating experience. You'll receive a noncommittal communiqué that neither accepts you nor rejects you outright but, instead, assigns you to a nerve-racking limbo. A friend of ours was waitlisted, and the letter she received read like the one that follows:

Dear Ms. Zura:

This letter may be the most frustrating of all to receive. It does not offer you admission to the Master of Business Administration Program at Western University, nor does it tell you that we cannot offer you a place in the class of 1994, nor does it tell you that we cannot offer you admission. It is a "waitlist" letter.

While your application to Western was strong, the number of candidates to whom we would like to offer admission exceeds the number of places available. If you are interested in accepting a place on the waitlist, we will review your file along with those of other waitlisted applicants in early July. Feel free to add any new information to your file that you would like us to take into consideration; please address it to Melina Watkins, Assistant Director of Admissions. I would also advise you to complete the GAPSFAS; if you are admitted from the waitlist and require financial aid, having completed this material will accelerate the process.

Candidates on the waitlist are not ranked. As a result, we are unable to tell you your position within the pool of waitlisted applicants, nor can we estimate your chances of being admitted. I can assure you, however, that your file will be given another detailed review and that you will receive the results of that review by mid-July.

We hope that you will accept a place on the GSB waitlist; to do so, please return the enclosed card by May 1.

I apologize for prolonging the admissions process, but please know that you are still a highly competitive candidate for admission.

Best regards,

Marcia Covey
Director of Admissions

If you are waitlisted, there is not, unfortunately, a great deal you can do to hasten the decision-making process. Additional openings in the class are usually made available when other people who have received offers of admission decline. The best advice we can give you is to keep in touch with the school. Don't nag the admissions staff, but let them know of the sincerity of your interest through the occasional phone call to an admissions committee member. In your phone call, tell the admissions office representative that you would be glad to come to campus for a supplementary interview. In addition, you may want to bolster your case for admission by sending the school an update on your professional activities in the months since you first submitted your application. An extra letter of recommendation from a strategically chosen, eloquent source might also be of help.

Schools are often vague about your position on their waitlist. As a result, you need to decide the latest time by which you can afford to rearrange your life to accommodate *their* schedule. Some people push this to the extreme. After spending three months on Harvard's waitlist, our friend Patty decided to head off to Kellogg. Two days after school had started there, she received a call from Harvard. Classes had not yet begun in Cambridge, and they wanted to know if she was still interested in the admissions offer. Patty packed her bags and moved. Situations like this are the exception rather than the rule, but they do happen. At most programs, admissions offers can be extended right until school starts.

Andy, another friend of ours, was recently accepted to Harvard from the waitlist. His story is an excellent example of the kind of proactive steps you might take to get yourself off the waitlist. After graduating from U.C. Berkeley, he spent two years working for Intel in Silicon Valley. He then spent the next two years in Africa as a Peace Corps volunteer. When Andy returned to the States, he went back to Intel and eventually applied to business school. Although he was waitlisted first time around, Andy kept in touch with Harvard's admissions committee. When he called to check on the progress of the waitlist, the assistant director of admissions asked him to send the admissions committee some information updating them on what he had been up to since he originally completed his application. Andy did them one better, crafting two articulate letters and a work-update summary, which he submitted for review. Less than a week after he sent the following supplementary material, Andy was admitted to the school.

The first of these letters was sent to the Director of Admissions.

Dear Ms. Johnson:

My conversation this Tuesday with Ms. Williams regarding my pending admission to Eastern inspired me to write this letter to you. As a recent admittee to your waitlist, I would like to discuss with you my attending the Eastern Business School this September. As you understand, business in the coming century will be extremely different from that of the last one. The fundamental shifts and restructuring are already profound: Instead of insulated multimarkets, the world will be one market; language and cultural challenges are going to be more prevalent in day-to-day business affairs; change and constant innovation will be an operating style rather than a goal; and successful business leaders are going to have to be team-oriented and cooperative in their approach to conducting business.

Since you are the person at the Eastern Business School most responsible for selecting a diverse class of tomorrow's leaders, I want to communicate to you that I have been following these trends carefully. I have committed the last several years to developing skills that will enable me to achieve my long-term vision and to provide genuine, serious leadership in the 21st century. As an undergraduate at U.C. Berkeley, my studies in engineering enabled me to develop the broad set of technical, analytical reasoning skills that will be necessary to succeed in the coming decades. Teaching a public speaking class enabled me to sharpen my abilities to speak and motivate others. My work in Silicon Valley has given me experience in management as well as in developing a real-world sense of the technologies that are going to be pervasive in our lives. Recognizing the coming globalization of industry, I spent several years developing small businesses and providing venture capital to entrepreneurs with the Peace Corps in Africa, where I gained a real appreciation for the cultural complexities and savoir faire that will be necessary to succeed in the global marketplace (I can now speak five languages valid on four different continents, shared by almost 2 billion people). As a result of this deliberate and continuous education, I have spent my early 20s assembling a broad set of skills that I am convinced every successful CEO will need in the coming years.

In addition to preparing for the future, I have focused the last few years upon developing a vision of what I want to achieve in the coming decades and beyond. My grand ambition—simply phrased— is to build and lead a global company. Having worked in Asia and Africa and seen the communications needs there, the arena in which I will focus my efforts is (wireless) communications. My two years at Eastern Business School will enable me to refine this vision and give it the critical attention and rigorous analysis that it deserves and needs (with the help, of course, of classmates, professors, field studies, and the Cook Library).

A vision lacks merit unless it stands upon a strong foundation of values: a genuine desire to help one's fellow man and society, sincerity and honesty of purpose, a willingness to work with others rather than to work against them, and the ability to add real value to one's profession and work. I have always integrated these values into my work and plan to remain true to them. Gaining foreign work experience through the U.S. Peace Corps—helping to develop small businesses and cooperatives in a part of the world where it really mattered—was an example of my commitment to these beliefs.

A vision also lacks merit if it cannot be achieved. And that has always been my hallmark: a drive and energy that has enabled me to attain every major goal I have ever set for myself. A great idea is nothing more than a good idea brilliantly executed. And that's why most of my ideas have become great ones.

I have taken a sober, long-term view of where our world and industries are headed and of my place in them. The challenges for my generation's leadership are going to be complex ones. The model under which we will be operating will be quite different from those we could have imagined as recently as a decade ago. These challenges will require serious, rigorous preparation for tomorrow's leaders; that is why I want to study at the Eastern Business School. The Eastern case method is the most rigorous and disciplined approach to management education in the world. Eastern provides superior preparation for its students so that they can achieve their long-term ambitions; one needs only to look at the track record of entrepreneurship and leadership in industry exhibited by Eastern graduates. I am also reassured by the fact that Eastern shares my view of a changing world and a business environment in flux, a fact that is reflected by the school's work on the new Leadership and Learning curriculum.

I spent several days at the Eastern campus last December—visiting classes, speaking with students, meeting professors, examining the resources of the Cook Library, learning about the new curriculum and Eastern's vision of management education for the future—and was convinced that I have much to contribute to the Eastern Business School and much to gain from spending two serious years there.

Attending the Eastern Business School will be a formidable challenge and an incredible opportunity to prepare myself for the leadership challenges of the 21st century. I am convinced that it is the next step in my continuous education toward achieving my long-term goals; I hope to become a member of the Eastern community and that we can work together to provide the global marketplace with the strong, dynamic leadership it deserves in the coming decades.

I will contact you soon in order to follow up on this letter and discuss my attendance at Eastern this fall.

Sincerely,

Andrew Friar

Andy's second letter and the accompanying work-update summary were sent to the Assistant Director.

Dear Ms. Williams:

This letter is a follow-up to our phone discussion of last week. As you instructed, I am enclosing an update of my work history since I applied to the Eastern Business School last fall. After returning from the Peace Corps last November, I moved to the San Francisco Bay area and began investigating various opportunities. Since my long-term ambition is to build and lead a global company, I decided to pursue opportunities that would further develop my skills in achieving that goal before attending Eastern. After considerable thought, I was persuaded to return to my previous company, Intel. The overriding factor in my decision was the scope of responsibilities they decided to offer me: In addition to normal product line marketing responsibilities, I am chairing a divisional task force that is seeking to redesign some key elements of the way in which we do business. I thought that the responsibilities of this position would be a good opportunity to gain the perspective and skills that will aid me in my future ambitions.

As I mentioned on the phone, I still believe that the Eastern Business School offers me the best possible preparation for the challenges of leading a company in the coming decades. I spent several days at the Eastern campus last fall—visiting classes, speaking with students, meeting professors, understanding the new Leadership and Learning curriculum—and became convinced that not only do I have much to contribute to Eastern, but that it will be the ideal place for me to hone my talents, to give rigorous analysis to my long-term plans, and to prepare for the challenges of leading and managing a company in the coming century.

Ms. Williams, I am excited to have been admitted to the waiting list and look forward to joining you in Boston in September.

Sincerely,

Andrew Friar

WORK-HISTORY UPDATE

HISTORY

JUNE 1989	Received degrees from U.C. Berkeley
JUNE 1989–AUGUST 1989	Traveled throughout Southeast Asia
JUNE 1991–NOV. 1993	Small Business Development/Venture Capital Programs Volunteer, U.S. Peace Corps
DEC. 1993–JAN. 1994	Returned to USA, spent time with my family, moved back to San Francisco, and began investigating several work opportunities

CURRENT WORK

Job Title: Staff Marketing Manager
Company: Intel Corporation
Location: Santa Clara, CA

Responsibilities

- Worldwide product-marketing activities of a semiconductor product line
- Launching new products into the marketplace
- Defining future product offerings
- Chairman of divisional business process reengineering task force

Long-Term Plans/Ambitions

- I want to build and lead a global high-technology company.
- I have become experienced in building business organizations, giving them focus and definition, and assisting a group in its efforts to develop a vision and achieve its objectives.
- I want to be a leader in the wireless communications field.
- The telecommunications opportunities in Asia and Africa are enormous. Having lived and worked in both of these areas, I have been able to study the markets up close and lay the seeds for future projects (I can now speak five languages that span four continents and are shared by 2 billion people).

Why am I a compelling candidate?

- I have a vision of what I want to achieve over the coming decades.
- I have spent my early 20s developing the skills and talents that are essential for achieving my goals.
- I have values that are essential to operating in an international business environment: honesty, integrity, the ability to cooperate and work with others, a desire to add real value to one's profession and society, and an appreciation for other cultures and work styles.
- I have the ability to implement and execute successfully the strategies needed to achieve my goals; I have demonstrated this repeatedly throughout my career, at every level of difficulty.

Why do I want to study at the Eastern Business School?

- It has the most rigorous and disciplined approach to management education in the world.

- It is the best management education program for the training of future entrepreneurs and CEOs.

- Eastern grads have a track record of entrepreneurship and leadership in industry that is unequaled.

- Eastern shares my view of a changing world and a business environment in flux, a fact that is illustrated by the school's new Leadership and Learning curriculum; I respect its ability to look into the future and to prepare for it.

- My two years at Eastern Business School will enable me to refine my vision and give it the critical attention and rigorous analysis that it deserves.

- I spent several days at Eastern last December—visiting classes, speaking with students, meeting professors, learning about the new curriculum—and became convinced that I have much to contribute to Eastern and much to gain by spending two years there.

As you can tell from his material, Andy is a pretty focused guy. He has a strong sense of purpose and used this opportunity to emphasize his direction to two key admissions decision makers. Not only did Andy want to go to business school, he wanted to attend one specific program; he makes this very clear to Ms. Johnson and Ms. Williams in his letters. Whereas a phone call is a one-time experience, sending a letter provides material that can be added to your records and passed from one admissions officer to another. In developing this detailed follow-up material, Andy made an influential addition to his admissions file.

Just as in the application essays themselves, it is important in communiqués such as Andy's to tell an admissions committee why you think there is a good match between your background and interests and their specific academic program. Andy also identified some of the current "hot topics" in management education, such as globalization, and used them effectively in his writing. In addition, notice his tone; it is confident and self-assured, something business schools like to see. Andy had clearly thought a lot about these issues: Having spent two years living in a mud hut in Africa, he had plenty of time for reflection! In all seriousness, though, if you're going to put together an "escape from the waitlist" campaign of your own, take some hints from Andy. Try not to let the uncertainty of the situation unnerve you. Seize the offensive.

DEFERRAL

The fourth and final option is deferred admission. Some applicants are asked to defer their admission to a later, specified date. When this happens, the school is usually acting in your best interest (you may or may not agree)—they think you will get more out of the program once you have significant work experience. One example is a friend of ours from college who applied to a top-ten business school during his senior year at Stanford and was granted deferred admission. Admission was contingent upon his working for two years in his industry of choice; if he did so, he was guaranteed a spot in the class that began in the fall of 1991, two years later.

In other cases, you may be able to defer your admission by request. This is extremely tricky, however; many schools are reluctant to grant such requests and only do so in unusual cases. This is not to say it's impossible. We have had several friends who have successfully deferred at different high-caliber MBA programs. But if you're going to attempt to defer your admission, you'll need to present a well-developed case that explains your interest in deferring, an interest that, ideally, will make you an even better qualified candidate for your MBA program of choice by the time you show up.

Eric, an old friend, took this approach and was able to defer at Stanford, Harvard, and Berkeley. At the time, he was living in California, while his fiancée was living in New Jersey. The two of them had carried on a transcontinental courtship for five years. Eric was able to convince admissions directors that another year of work would make him a better contributor at their respective programs. By deferring a year and working from a home office in New Jersey, he argued, he and his bride-to-be would be able to see what life was like when together on a day-to-day basis. The irony was that, after his ardent efforts to arrange deferrals at these different institutions, Eric ended up attending MIT's Sloan School of Management the next fall—as did his wife, who applied during the year they lived together in New Jersey. By the way, the official stance of most MBA programs is that they evaluate couples as individuals, not as a pair. We would argue, however, that they can't help but take "couple status" into consideration, especially if you make it known in your application or your interview that your partner is applying. We suggest you do. It worked for Eric and Margaret, it worked for us, and it could certainly work for you.

In addition, as Eric and Margaret's story illustrates, it is just fine to request a deferral based on personal reasons. It can be tough to put your normal life on hold for two years, and moving to a new city can be a hassle, especially for those with spouses or significant others. Throwing children into the equation can make things even more complex. Admissions committees can be remarkably understanding at times. The important thing is that you make your argument for deferral articulately.

Our friend Joe was initially waitlisted, but in time, he was granted admission. Joe, however, was a talented software engineer and also had been offered the opportunity to join a promising start-up company. He decided to request a deferral and wrote this letter:

Dear Ms. Johnson:

Thank you for taking the time to meet with me last week to discuss my candidacy for the Eastern Business School. I was glad to have the opportunity to share my perspective with you, and I'm excited by the prospect of attending Eastern. As you know, I applied only to Eastern and this acceptance means a great deal to me.

I'm sending you this fax to follow up on a conversation with Ms. Williams about the possibility of deferring my admission until next fall. This possibility was first raised by Ms. Williams on the sixth of August, and I took that to the Insight Systems International board meeting on the tenth.

When approached with the possibility that I might receive a deferred admission, Insight Systems came up with an intriguing offer. Insight informed me that they would be interested in hiring me for a year to focus on several specific near-term projects, including leading the development team for the company's next version of their current product Visi-Fax and continuing the negotiations for international distribution that I began on my trip to Asia this spring. These responsibilities would give me a chance to gain additional hands-on management skills and to experience the excitement of working with a small start-up venture.

I feel that I will be able to offer more to a classroom at the Eastern Business School after a year of general management experience at Insight Systems. This in no way diminishes my desire to attend Eastern, but rather reflects my interest in taking advantage of an opportunity that will make the business school experience more valuable for both me and my classmates.

Sincerely,

Joseph Lu

Joe made a good case for himself. In this letter, he not only reemphasized his interest in eventually attending business school, he also illustrated in detail the ways in which the experience at Insight Systems would make him a stronger candidate for the program. To Joe's delight, he was deferred. The letter he received looked like this:

Dear Mr. Lu:

I am pleased to inform you that the Admissions Board has voted to offer you Deferred Admission to the Eastern Graduate School of Business Administration. We have reserved a place for you in the MBA Program with the class entering in September of next year. Admission is recognition of your record of accomplishment and potential for success in both the academic and professional worlds. Congratulations!

Enrollment in the MBA Program is an opportunity to join a community of students from around the globe in sharing a stimulating and rigorous educational experience. Deferred admission gives you time to develop further your administrative talents and judgment by obtaining additional work experience before returning to school. Our goal is to help you make the most of your two years at the Eastern Business School. We hope you will accept this offer and join us next fall.

Our offer is a firm commitment, provided that you continue working for an additional year and that you report briefly on this work experience using an update form we will send you. Should you decide to change jobs in the course of the next year, you must seek prior approval from the MBA Admissions Board.

Margaret Williams, Assistant Director of Admissions, will be happy to answer any questions you may have. You may reach her by telephone at 617-555-1076.

We look forward to hearing from you and to welcoming you to the Eastern Business School community.

Sincerely,

Louisa Johnson
Chairman

Joe spent an extremely busy year at Insight Systems and thoroughly enjoyed the experience. In fact, he was so happy in his position at Insight that by the next spring, he was wondering if he should try to defer his admission to Eastern for yet another year. Although he knew it was unlikely that he would be granted an additional deferral, Joe thought he might as well try. His second request for deferred admission follows:

Dear Ms. Johnson:

As you know, last fall I accepted deferred admission to the MBA program in order to spend the year as Director of Research and Development at Insight Systems International, a start-up software company. As the fall fast approaches and the time comes to leave for Boston, I find myself facing the following dilemma.

Insight Systems has turned out to be an extraordinary opportunity for entrepreneurial involvement, and it is succeeding in the marketplace far beyond my expectations. I still want to attend the Business School. Indeed, my daily experience reinforces to me the value of an Eastern MBA. My dilemma is whether the time for the MBA is sooner rather than later.

In the past year, I have managed Insight Systems' engineering team through the development of two products that are crucial to our company's success. I'm currently attempting to balance R&D, marketing, and financial responsibilities for these products, applications that should give us the opportunity to dominate our niche across multiple computer platforms. The choices are vast, and we really only get one chance to do this right.

While performing these jobs, I serve as the lightning rod for conflicts between marketing and R&D, our chief negotiator of deals and strategic alliances with other companies, our venture capital chaser, perforce the CFO, and the Insight Systems' softball team's third baseman. Each week brings a new challenge and a new opportunity to learn and grow. Not insignificantly, Insight Systems also holds the potential to reward me financially.

I would appreciate the chance to discuss my situation with you and will call next week to ask for an appointment.

Thank you for your consideration.

Sincerely,

Joseph Lu

Again, Joe reaffirmed the amount he was learning at this start-up venture. From the degree of cross-functional experience he was getting, it must have been clear to the admissions office that he would both learn more himself and make a greater contribution to the classroom environment were he allowed to continue at Insight Systems. Joe was actually granted deferral a second time. By the summer, however, Joe decided that despite everything he was learning at the company, he would be interested in returning to school that fall. He joined Eastern's entering class in September of 1992.

As you can see from Joe's story, although many MBA programs will discourage you from doing so, it is possible to postpone attending school once you've been admitted. The key is to make a compelling argument that shows how your plans in the interim period will not only enable you to get more from the business school experience, but also help you give more to the community of students with whom you'll spend those two years.

ANALYZING YOUR CHOICES

Once you've heard yea, or nay, or maybe from the schools to which you've applied, it's time to do some careful thinking. At this point, you may feel ecstatic, lukewarm, or disappointed about the choices you face. Remember, however, that no amount of research you do up front can make you fully aware of all the strengths and shortcomings of a particular MBA program. Our friend Rachel was initially disappointed about the results of her application efforts. She had been admitted to only one school, Columbia, and she had her heart set on Kellogg. Once she discovered that she had been denied admission there, she became fixated on the belief that no other program would provide the strong marketing focus that she thought Kellogg would. She got over this in time, however, and eventually decided to attend Columbia. Today, she will tell you that her two years at Columbia were among the most extraordinary years of her life. She is now an account manager at a top advertising agency in New York and would not trade her graduate experience for anything.

Even though analysis of the different programs won't tell you everything, it is worth a detailed effort. You're about to spend two years of your life and a bushel of money on this educational adventure. You're making a purchase. Think about what you're buying. When evaluating a program, ask yourself questions like the following:

Academic Strengths

- Is the school strong in my academic areas of preference?
- Is it strong in those areas in which I need help?
- Do recruiters know of these strengths?
- How many of my classes will be taught by seasoned professors? By rookies?
- Is the school able to attract top professors and interesting visitors from the business community?
- Does the school allow people to place out of introductory classes in fields in which they have significant prior experience?

Alumni

- How large is the alumni network?
- Is the alumni network national or international?
- Is the alumni network a strong, cooperative one or a loosely affiliated collection of individuals?

Character

- Is the program competitive or cooperative in spirit?
- Is the program more quantitative or qualitative?
- How are students evaluated?
- Does the program feature more individual or group-oriented work? Which do I prefer?
- How large is the entire class?
- Are classes broken down into sections? If so, how large are they, and for how long are students assigned to these sections?
- How much interaction will I have with my professors?

Expenses/Financial

- What will the program cost me?
- Can I get a better financial aid program elsewhere?

- If so, am I willing to go to a school that is not my first choice if the cost will be lower?

Geography

- Is the school located in an area in which I don't mind spending two years?
- Does the location of the program give me an opportunity to explore a new part of the country?
- If I'm interested in studying overseas during my time at business school, does the school have an overseas program or an affiliation with an institution that does?
- What is the weather like? Can I put up with a frigid six-month winter, or do I require constant sun to maintain my sanity?
- If the school is located in an urban area, what do I think of the social, cultural, and recreational opportunities the city presents?
- If the school is located in a rural area, what do I think of the social and recreational opportunities the town presents? Is there enough in the way of "culture" to satisfy me?

Personal

- Would my spouse or significant other mind living in this area for two years?
- Could my spouse or significant other relocate with his or her current employer, or would he or she need to find another job?
- How is the social life? Do single people have much opportunity or time to meet and date others either within or outside the academic community?

Recruiting

- Which companies recruit at the school?
- Do many potential employers interview on campus, or will I have to go to them?
- If I do need to travel for recruiting, how easy or difficult is it for me to do that?

- Do those companies that recruit on campus represent industries that are of interest to me?
- What resources does the school make available to those students who are interested in doing an independent job search rather than going through the on-campus recruiting process?
- What percentage of the program's students have jobs upon graduation?

Reputation

- How important to me is a school's prestige or "brand equity"?
- Does the program have a regional, national, or international reputation?
- If it has a stronger presence in one area of the country or part of the world, is this where I want to live after school?

YOUR FINAL DECISION

As the preceding questions suggest, the choice is an intensely personal one. Think these issues over carefully. Go back and review the work you did researching your target markets and developing a personal positioning campaign. Look at the strength of the match between your interests and background and the school that you are considering. See Appendix F for a chart to help structure your thinking.

When we made our decision, our thinking process went something like this:

- **Location** Having spent his life in California, Phil wanted to see a new part of the country for two years, an idea that also appealed to Carol.
- **Reputation** Both of us were interested in attending a top-notch program with a strong, international alumni base because we didn't know where in the world we might want to land after business school and wanted to have the flexibility that attending a visible, well-known program would provide.
- **Curriculum** We were both interested in general management and marketing, and Phil knew he wanted to beef up his knowledge of finance.

- **Recruiting** We wanted a school that had a decent on-campus re-cruiting program, but this was not the most important issue. As high-tech people, we understood that many of the companies in this industry would not recruit at business schools anyway—we would be looking for them.

- **Class Size** While we inherently preferred a program with a smaller class size, we were willing to yield on this point if a program met our other criteria.

- **Financial Cost** We also decided that it was worth spending the money to do this right. Although we cringed at the idea of taking on significant debt, we believed that, in the long run, attending the best school to which we were admitted would help us command salaries that could be used to pay off the debt quickly.

Again, the choice is a personal one and will involve making trade-offs. Attending business school is an investment in a package of goods and services, an investment that will have both short-term and long-term effects and benefits. Our advice is to make the investment that you think will give you the greatest return over time.

Remember, if you have been admitted to *any* of the top business schools, you deserve a pat on the back. Thousands of people applied; *you* got in. In your situation, no choice you make is going to be a bad choice. At any of these good schools, you are assured a top-notch education and an intelligent, interesting group of peers. Analyze the options you have, make your decision, and go change the world.

12

From the Horse's Mouth: Advice from Top Admissions Directors

The price of wisdom is above rubies.

Bible—Job 28:18

To be able to give you insights from the kind of people who will be reviewing your applications, we spoke with three influential decision makers: Linda Baldwin, the Director of Admissions for the UCLA Andersen Graduate School of Management; Marie Mookini, the Director of Admissions for the Stanford University Graduate School of Business; and Jon Megibow, the Director of Admissions for the University of Virginia's Darden School.

In selecting these three schools, we were looking to provide you with some variety. Stanford is a private West Coast school. Whereas UCLA is also on the West Coast, it is a public institution. UVA's Darden School is the East Coast representative and, like UCLA, is a public school.

We asked Linda, Marie, and Jon a number of difficult questions. Their responses make up the rest of this chapter. When you review their answers, you'll notice that there are some areas in which their opinions differ, such as the value of the evaluative interview. However, you'll also see that there are common themes that begin to emerge in the admissions directors' responses, such as the degree to which MBA programs value leadership skills in applicants or the importance of selecting recommenders who know you well and will write specific, insightful recommendations. While these three people cannot speak for the entire community of MBA admissions committee members, it's worth taking particular note of the common themes and thinking about how you might address some of these issues in your application.

We recommend that you read the interviews included in this chapter early in the development of your personal positioning strategy. Many of the questions were specifically designed to push the respondents, to gather information that would help you to better understand what your "customers" are looking for. To develop a good marketing campaign, you need to be familiar with the needs and preferences of your target market. Taking the time to review these interviews early in the application season will help you to approach the process with the kind of market intelligence you need to craft effective, marketing-oriented applications.

1. What qualities would you like to see more of in candidates?

Linda Baldwin, UCLA   I want to see strong academic skills, and that comes through the information I get on paper via transcripts and GMATs. But beyond academics, I want to see how individuals have demonstrated their ability to perform and to take charge—to lead. We're looking to see how they manage their work lives, as well as their lives outside of the workplace. What type of roles do they take on in these activities, and what do they get excited about? I like to see whether they are action-oriented people who take the initiative and how they handle structured and unstructured situations.

   With the promising applicants, there's an unfolding that occurs. If you look at their progression, you see that they've accomplished certain things and have taken on leadership roles. They have a pattern of achievement, and it's that pattern that I'm looking for.

   Also, I want to see strong verbal and written communication skills. Through recommendations, we learn what people have to say about candidates' ability to interrelate with others. What they (the candidates) write in their applications and what they say in interviews helps complete the picture.

   Finally, I'm looking for applicants who want to do more than just live for themselves—that's a big one for us. You like to see a balance of giving as well as receiving—how they plan to utilize the resources here, but also how they plan to give back, how they will contribute to our environment.

Marie Mookini, Stanford   Every school wants more smart people, more thoughtful people, more leaders. I think that many of our applicants exhibit those kind of qualities, whether latent or well developed. But the applicant's responsibility is to describe those qualities in such vivid detail that when the admissions officer reads the file, she can't come to any other conclusion but, "Wow! This person is going to be a great leader and is the kind of person we want at our business school." Students should strive to be thoughtful and descriptive in their presentations—don't sell yourself short!

Jon Megibow, Darden I'd like to see more evidence of successful risk taking. One of the attractive qualities about so many people who apply to graduate business school is their careful planning and forethoughtfulness. Everything seems to fit together with an awful lot of consideration for the future. What we don't see enough of are people who have assessed situations and taken paths less traveled. To some extent, many people who are successful in their application to business school are more mature than their age would predict. Some of the downside that can come with this maturity is too much caution, not enough knocking over the chessboard, rather than being experts in how to play the game.

2. How may your criteria for admissions have changed over the past few years? Do you seek different qualities in candidates today than you did five years ago?

Linda I think that, today, we look for similar qualities in different ways. We used to look primarily at academics to develop an understanding of a candidate's level of initiative, ability to solve problems creatively, and the like. But now, we look more broadly to see how the person seems to master his life in total. We try to understand how he uses *all* of his time, whether at school, work, or outside of work.

We also evaluate their global experiences; that wasn't a big factor in the past. We look to see what knowledge they have of other places, what experience they've had interacting with people who are different than they are, what languages they may have mastered or what overseas work or travel they may have done. With the increasingly global nature of business today, those are all important issues that hadn't been looked at as much.

We're also more attuned to candidates' excitement about change, their ability to face change and adapt to it. We look closely at individuals who say they've been involved in changing environments and how they perceive and deal with such change.

Finally, given the rising level of interest in entrepreneurship amongst our applicants, we are interested in hearing from prospective students who have started their own businesses, as well as from those that profess a desire to do so in the future.

Marie Our admissions criteria haven't changed a lot over the years. There are three main requirements for admission to Stanford. The first is academic performance: We want people who are intelligent and have a real commitment to the learning process. The second criterion is one that most business schools share, and that is "demonstrated management potential." This is broadly defined as people who have managed, who have demonstrated their leadership abilities, and people who maybe haven't done so yet but show promise. For those in the latter camp, we look for the personal qualities that are conducive to management and leadership. The third criterion is diversity. We're looking for not only ethnic and international diversity, but also a range of different perspectives and personal qualities that will add to the GSB community. So in general, the criteria really haven't changed. However, the applicant pool obviously changes, as you get a different set of applicants every year.

Jon Every year our criteria change slightly, and the changes are in response to internal issues and concerns. The faculty may say, "We need more people with technical experience or education" or "We seem to be undervaluing local talent in our headlong rush to be perceived as a nationally competitive MBA program; let's give more weight to in-state status." They might suggest, "We need to improve our positioning vis-à-vis other MBA programs in the rankings, so let's put a greater value on standardized test scores."

Those are hypothetical examples, but they are characteristic of the kind of issues that might be raised. Each year, there are changes like this that tend to be driven by demographics or by other perceptions on the part of the faculty. At the same time, there are market forces at play. One of the things that strikes me as particular to this year's entering class—and I suspect it will also be true for next year's class—is that we're starting to see the impact in admissions of a lousy economy. This means that the people who are applying to the MBA program don't have the same quality of work experience as applicants may have had in the past. They were forced by circumstances to accept employment in positions that afforded them much more limited opportunities for distinction. As a result, we're having to look for evidence elsewhere of some of the characteristics that we value in candidates.

3. How much time do you spend on each application in total?

Linda It varies, though I would say that an experienced reader will probably spend 20 to 40 minutes in total per file. On average, three people read each application. We also do a two-page evaluation of the applicant after we've reviewed his or her materials.

Marie It depends. If people write ten pages, it's going to take us a little longer to read than someone who only devotes a page and a half to telling us about his or her career goals. On average, however, we probably spend 20 to 30 minutes per file per reader. Two people read each application, and in some cases three. All the admitted students' files have been read by three people.

Jon I would say between 40 minutes and an hour.

4. What influence, if any, do family contacts or legacy status have on your admissions process?

Linda It really doesn't have much of an impact on the admissions process. We're getting increasing numbers of legacy applicants here in California, but we can't let that be a factor. We look at what the *person* has done. We do ask a little bit about their family background, but that's more to see how prospective students perceive their roles as family members. Understanding our applicants' relationships with their families gives us a gauge of their emotional composition or profile. People who seem cold or distant may lead you to question how they would handle other collaborative, team-based relationships. If there is any true collaboration in life, it usually comes in a family. You're stuck with those people for a long time!

Marie There is no formal policy, but certainly it's something that we take into consideration. We're sensitive to family ties to the institution and certainly want to make a commitment to continuing those family traditions. So while there's nothing in writing, the "legacy relationship" is something we do take into consideration, just as we would the presence of siblings or spouses.

Jon That is just becoming an issue with Darden, as we are such a young school. Until 1974, we were only admitting about 70 to 80 people per year. We're just now getting to a point that enough of our graduates have children of an age to be applying to MBA programs that we're beginning to take the alumni relationship into account. Because the numbers are so small, as much as because we're concerned about the interest of our alumni, we do take legacy status into consideration. It is an issue very much in play when we make our selections. But since we're talking about no more than 2 to 3 percent of the entering class in any given year, while it is advantageous for a candidate to be the son or daughter of an alum, the numbers are so negligible that I don't think that it has a detrimental impact on the process as a whole.

Although there are many more applicants whose parents may have spent their undergraduate years at UVA, that affiliation doesn't come into play, largely because the parents of Darden applicants who went to UVA as undergraduates are making their financial contributions to the University as a whole, not to Darden.

5. Given that some companies (i.e., McKinsey & Company, Goldman Sachs, etc.) seem to be traditional feeders for your MBA program, how is an applicant from one of these firms viewed against other applicants in the pool?

Linda I think that those companies are fine feeders. However, if you're looking to say that they immediately assume some additional stature, I have to counter that we assess each applicant as she comes to us. We tend to look at those candidates and realize the type of rigorous training they've had and have a better understanding of what they've gone through. But though applicants from these companies may be more of a known quantity, they need to articulate what they've learned. We leave it to the candidates to express to us clearly what they have been able to achieve in those environments. For us to assume would be presumptuous.

Marie In general, our focus is more on the individual than on the company; we don't read files by company. Our aim is to get the best people. A lot of them do come out of the McKinseys and the Goldmans, but the focus really is on the individual and what he is going to bring to the GSB community. It certainly doesn't hurt or hinder the applicant—we know that these companies have done a wonderful job at skimming the best and the brightest out of the colleges. In a sense, they've really prescreened our applicants for us. These institutions *are* great feeders. They have a strong commitment to affirmative action, and I suspect that the criteria that they use for hiring is similar to the criteria that a lot of the top business schools use for admission. They're looking for smart, energetic people who are going to be the leaders of tomorrow and so are we; so our goals are in sync. It thus stands to reason that, in business schools, you're going to find a lot of people from those top companies.

Jon There's an incestuous relationship that exists between probably 100 to 200 companies and MBA programs. It's sort of like passing a hot potato back and forth. If you take a look at the schools that are most frequently mentioned as top tier, almost all of them are B-schools that exist in the context of a larger academic institution. And those larger universities tend to be feeders to those 100 to 200 prime recruiters of undergraduates; for example, somebody out of the University of Virginia's philosophy department will go to work for Morgan Stanley. These relationships have often been in place long before the MBA programs developed their own bonds with these companies. I would bet that two dozen colleges and universities in the United States probably account for 75 to 80 percent of the students that this pool of companies hires out of undergraduate schools. And then those 100 to 200 companies train those graduates of the 24 schools, and at the end of two years, those people reshuffle themselves. They occasionally go back to their original baccalaureate institution, but more often than not, they go to a different one of those 24 schools. Then, there is a final shifting back and forth where, having completed an MBA, people go to work for another one of those 100 companies, and not necessarily the same one they came from. It is an unfortunate situation, but it is very much a country club. And if you get in at the front end to one of those 24 schools and do well, it is significantly easier for you to make the transition into and out of the next three stages.

On a related issue, we hear an awful lot about the value of full-time work experience prior to getting an MBA, and I think there's some pedagogical truth to that, particularly in a case-method program. The top-tier schools tacitly set a hurdle of several years of full-time work experience. The real reason behind this requirement, however, is that often those 100 companies won't hire someone without full-time work experience. Thus, the selection process is driven as much by the demands of those 100 companies as it is by internal pedagogical and philosophical issues. And that's something that's one of those deep, dark secrets that both companies and schools are unwilling to acknowledge. Until fairly recently, we stopped admitting undergraduates, not because they were unqualified, but because they came with the expectation that they would have the same employment opportunities as someone with full-time work experience. And regardless of how well they did, they were not afforded those opportunities.

6. Who serves on your admissions committee—students? administrators? alumni? professors? others?

Linda We include students, professional admissions officers, alumni, and faculty in the admissions process. Each year, a group of no more than ten second-year students go through a two-month admissions training course. Our admissions officers serve as their mentors; these students do rotations with different admissions staffers to gain the benefit of their insights and perspective. As I mentioned, our admissions process entails an approximately two-page write-up, and students are actively involved in preparing these summaries.

Our admissions officers come from a number of various areas. We have one individual on the admissions committee who has been primarily focused on the international area. This person has a master's degree, speaks about five languages, has done extensive travel, and brings a global perspective to the table. We have an MBA grad who spent time on Wall Street and in public relations. We have an individual who has been in the admissions field for about 20 years at several top-notch MBA programs. Another one of our staff members has extensive experience in the area of minority-program development. She understands the perspective of different communities and ethnic groups, which has been a valuable asset for us.

We also involve alums—they're typically individuals who have been trained prior to graduation, and there are about six of them. With regard to the faculty, the professors of some of our specialized programs have some input as well; for example, our arts management and international management professors lend a voice in the selection of students for these focused variations on the UCLA MBA.

Marie We rely primarily on professional admissions-staff members. Also, the director of the MBA program, a faculty member at the business school, will read the files of the recommended "admits." Unlike some other institutions, we don't involve students or alumni in the decision-making process. The assumption is that the admissions staff is a professional organization and that we've been charged with the responsibility of selecting the best and the brightest out of the applicant pool. There's also a sense that there is a greater amount of control and consistency in hiring professionals to do the admissions job.

Jon We have two admissions committees that have advisory roles, rather than roles directly in assessment and selection. We have a student admissions committee, comprised of four first-year and four second-year students that help us plan strategy; for example, they think about what we need to do to be more attractive to people in terms of our host activities or our recruiting events off campus. The four second-year students, along with approximately two dozen other second-year students, serve as student interviewers. They will do probably about a sixth of the interviews. We also have a faculty committee that is comprised of about a half dozen senior, tenured faculty members that oversees the admissions process. They ask questions about why we do what we do and how successful we have been. They give us, to some extent, our marching orders. They might suggest, "We would like to see a target of no fewer than 30 percent women for the entering class" or "At least 15 percent of the class should be underrepresented minorities." They'll raise questions about changes in the population of the entering class. "It seems to us," they might say, "that there are a disproportionate number of people from the nonprofit sector this year. Was that intentional? If it was, what were the motives of the admissions committee?"

In terms of assessment, there are five of us on staff who conduct interviews and read applications. My four colleagues do an initial screening of every application. Then the application comes to me. I'll read the application and, if I concur with the initial decision, I'll make a final decision and a letter will go out. If I have any questions, I will send the application back and try to get a third opinion. If the decision that I have reached or that my colleagues have made falls so far outside of what the faculty believes are typical or normal standards for the decision-making process, I'll pass the application along with my decision to the chair of the faculty committee. The chair will review it, sometimes share it with other members of the committee, and then either concur with my decision or question it. If there are questions, we then sit down and deliberate.

7. *Many students who have pursued pre-MBA career paths may not have had the opportunity to manage others; yet management potential is high on the list of attributes that MBA programs are seeking. For students in this position, how would you suggest they resolve this dilemma when writing their applications?*

Linda   I think that managerial potential is just that . . . *potential.* To form an opinion of an applicant's level of potential, we look at the activities in which she's taken a leadership role since her undergraduate years. What experience has she had motivating and organizing individuals, managing projects, delegating authority, and communicating her thoughts and goals to others? This sort of experience can be had in a number of different ways: It doesn't all have to come from running a business. You can get it in not-for-profit, in clubs and organizations, or through managing a family. You can get it while you're a teen idol in Japan or an Olympic gold medalist, someone who doesn't have "traditional experience" but has shown her motivation and leadership potential serving as the leader of a group of individuals and meeting with people in the corporate sector to raise funds. Summer jobs can be a good signal of this potential as well, a progression of work experiences from summer to summer in which the individual may lay a knowledge foundation at one place, then seek a position that includes even greater responsibilities at the next. You don't want to narrow things so much that it all has to be done at Bain or Merrill Lynch. We hear every fall from amazing people with extraordinary backgrounds. They don't all have to have worked on Wall Street for two years to have gotten these experiences.

Marie   As I mentioned, our second criterion for admission is "demonstrated management potential," and as some people have had management jobs, it's easy for them—through their resumes, through their recommendations—to tell us about those achievements. For the people who haven't yet had a chance to manage in the workplace, we look back to their undergraduate activities, because that's a good measure of early seeds of leadership. We look to leadership positions in clubs or in the Greek system, for example. Perhaps you were a Residential Advisor in your dormitory or were in student government. That's why we ask people to list their collegiate extracurricular activities, as it gives us a feeling for their proclivity for leadership. Recommendations are just as helpful. A manager might say, "Sam hasn't had a chance to lead a team or manage a project, but he's a person who would take off if we slapped that title across his forehead. He would command the respect of the team members and move them toward the goal." Reviewing the references, scanning the essays for the personal qualities and skills that are prerequisites for becoming a good manager and/or leader—all these things enable us to evaluate an applicant's managerial potential.

Jon   I think that there are two things that we would look at or two suggestions we would make. Sometimes individuals are very forethoughtful or premeditated in their pursuit of an MBA. They decide during undergraduate school that is where they want to go. After college, they might go to work for a Big Six accounting firm or a large manufacturing multinational where their opportunities to be decision makers and managers will be limited until they have been there for five years. With those people, we often won't give them serious consideration until they've paid their dues, until they've worked long enough to have some managerial experience. As a result, in every class, those people tend to be older rather than younger, slightly above rather than below the average age. They'll be those people who have followed the most safe professional path. To have spent two years at a Big Six accounting firm doing audits is just not enough, whereas two years managing your own start-up company is wonderful preparation for business school. At a Big Six firm, you have to have been there three, maybe four years to have had supervisory experience of other staff auditors, to have had some large audit supervision responsibilities, to have maybe even reached the point where you were starting to pitch some business.

We would raise similar questions with people who have completed the standard two-year analyst program. We also look for evidence in college of extracurricular management accomplishments. Those people who want to lead, who want to manage, will find or create the opportunities to do so. Many people who pursue those traditional paths seem to have cookie-cutter credentials in a lot of ways; so that is one way of discriminating among excellence.

8. What makes a good recommendation? What kinds of people do you think most often write effective recommendations?

Linda   A good recommendation is one that is specific and uses the format that we provide. In addition, the recommendation should include a letter that provides details about the applicant's accomplishments and achievements. I'm looking for a total assessment of the individual: how he works with others, how he has been challenged, how he has grappled with that challenge, and how he's changed over time. If a recommender can give me insights like that, then I'm in good shape. Writers should avoid using generic phrases like "natural born leader," "personable," and "great guy"—they don't really give us much to go on and certainly don't set you apart from everyone else. Give me more detail. Otherwise, the applicant is stuck in a pool with 3,000 other people who have used the same words, and I read 6,000 of these recommendations. Recommenders should strive to distinguish the individual by giving us the specifics. I don't mind reading a two- or three-page recommendation—those three-paragraph things sometimes do no more than say, "Hi, I got the letter and got it back to you." Those don't help me at all.

As to who you should ask to write your recommendations, if you've been out more than two years, make sure one comes from your manager—someone who knows you well, has seen your progress within your organization, and could make the decision to promote you. An academic reference is also a good addition, particularly if the applicant has been out of school for less than two years or if there is any doubt or question about the applicant's academic performance. If student leadership makes up a significant portion of the prospective student's leadership portfolio, then the individual should have a recommendation that relates to us how that person had an impact on campus or what special leadership attributes that person has. Choose your recommenders carefully—their words are worth a lot to us, and they can sing your praises in a way that you might not without sounding immodest. Finally, provide your recommenders with a cover letter that indicates why they were selected, as well as a clear explanation of what needs to be completed when. In addition, you may want to attach a resume.

Marie On the letters of reference form for Stanford, I've included a short letter to the recommender in which I say that what really helps us is for the recommender to give specific anecdotes about a candidate. Most people who apply are going to get references from people who like them and know them well. And typically, as you can imagine, 99 percent of the references are positive. They say, "John has been an asset to Company X, he's reliable, he's smart, he's been wonderful." We *know* that you're wonderful people, so a good recommendation will include specific anecdotes. "John was staffed on a project in which he did this, that, and the other." What also helps is when recommenders answer our question. This assumes that the recommender knows that applicant well enough to do that. So hint number two is to get a reference from someone who knows you well. It's fun and wonderful to get a letter from Al Gore or your senator, but in all likelihood, they don't know you, and, thus, it really doesn't help your candidacy at all. If you're at Goldman, don't go to the managing director; go to the associate with whom you work most closely. It's quite helpful for us to hear from people who not only know you but who have evaluated your work.

I also encourage the applicants to go and talk to their recommenders. You should be able to go to the person and say, "I'm applying to business school. This is what I plan to discuss in my essays, and I would really like for you to talk about the time when I did X, Y, and Z." Basically, I see the application like a jigsaw puzzle. The transcript and the essays are the bulk of the puzzle; the recommendations help complete the picture by complementing what we get from the applicant. If we're getting a feeling from the essays that the student is driven in a positive way, and we pick up the same themes in the recommendations, it all fits together. That's what admissions is all about—putting all the pieces of the puzzle together and seeing what you end up with. Once you have the coherent picture, you think to yourself, "How does this person match with some of the other applicants I've evaluated, and which combination of applicants would produce the most interesting and diverse GSB community?"

Jon Having read thousands of applications, this is the area where applicants are least perceptive about what they can do to leverage their chances for admission. Few people get recommendations from people who don't praise them to the sky. Those kinds of recommendations are easy to obtain; they're a dime a dozen. They often do absolutely nothing to further a candidate's prospects for admission. Letters of recommendation that are most valuable are those that are able to articulate the specific noteworthy characteristics of the candidate, rather than saying, "This person walks on water, this person does this, this person does that." Recommendations that are most helpful are able to talk about the character of the individuals, not just the capabilities and the accomplishments. It's just like what makes a good essay. It isn't simply talking about what you've accomplished, but why you've done it, therefore creating a sense of you as an individual, that somehow distinguishes you from that mass of other applicants.

Of course, you have a greater amount of control with the essays, as you are writing those yourself; but it is important to understand that this is what admissions officers are looking for. It's essential that you find a recommender who is capable, not just in terms of writing but in terms of communications skills, of relaying these ideas. The most effective recommenders are those with whom you have worked most closely, those with whom you have a relationship.

9. How do you recommend that students differentiate themselves from the pack?

Linda It's not something that you manipulate, but you can "take care of business" in a certain way, so that it ends up that you haven't left holes in your case. For the most part, we're advocating for you in this process. We're putting a case together, and if we don't have what we need to make a case, then the decision is not going to be favorable. Strong academics are clearly essential; before he applies to MBA programs, it is important that an individual step back, assess where his weaknesses are, and maybe take a course in the area. If calculus didn't work well for him early on, take a course at a community college, an extension or a four-year evening program and get an A. Go back and create a bit of what we call an alternate transcript. Be proactive in how you build your case. If you have shortcomings, address them. With reference to your extracurriculars and leadership, you don't have to be part of every club and organization. What we really want to see is what you thought was important and how you assumed a leadership role in those activities that were important to you. Applicants need to tell us what that role was—we can't surmise it. In writing about your managerial experiences, understand what is meant by "managerial" and try not to limit yourself to a business-context-only definition. Build a logical, complete argument in favor of your admission. The more we know, the easier it is for us to serve as advocates on your behalf.

Marie What I recommend is that our applicants begin by realizing that they are neat people! You've done some great things and should be proud of what you've accomplished. Describe yourself in vivid detail. Talk about the things that you care about most, because that is going to make you stand out. If you take some time to figure out what impassions you and describe them well, that's what will make you stand out. You don't need to have done something really exotic or esoteric to stand out in the pool, and that's what I want applicants to understand. There are a lot of people we admit who haven't done anything out of the ordinary, but the passion they bring to the job and to other activities is something that's going to carry over to the community here and really inspire others. The way you present things can make all the difference.

10. Are there any typical trite answers to your program's application or interview questions that you read or hear all too often?

Linda One of them is when they go too far—when they go back to high school. It's not necessary to dredge that deep into the past. I say, "Ugh—how far is this history going to take me?" I don't need a recitation of high school achievements. Another common weakness I see is when an application is too one-dimensional. It really does a disservice to the individual when he focuses only on work. I realize that might be ruling his life now, but he should not fixate there. Another thing that irks me is when they answer the "ethical dilemma" question without being asked it. You're thinking, "Where did that one come from?" Applicants love to do this.

"I take on too much responsibility" is yet another trite reply. On occasion, you also get people who recite their job description as a leadership role, which defeats the purpose of what our questions on this issue are all about. In addition, you often get people who try to fake you out concerning the types of community activities in which they're involved.

Marie I surveyed my staff on this: The one we consistently came up with was, "I'm a people person." Well so what? Tell us more. What does that mean?

People also cover mundane topics—parents as the subject of the "person who influenced your life" essay, for example. But you can turn something that is commonplace into writing that is extraordinarily interesting. Routine can be compelling if you tie it in well. It depends on you presenting your life in a descriptive, vivid way. If you give me specific anecdotes about how you've interacted with people or talk about an occasion where you had to confront your boss on a controversial issue, I can derive from that information that you are a "people person." Thus, there are trite topics as well as trite responses, but there are ways to make them less so.

The other common answer that we get in response to our question "Why do you want to come to Stanford Business School?" is "Because it's the best school." How are we the best for *you*?

Jon I've been rereading the applications of our matriculating students in anticipation of their arrival several weeks from now. I want to be able to know them by name, to talk with them about what they've done and who they are. We have four to five essays in which we try to give the applicants an opportunity to show us how multifaceted they are. These essays give candidates a chance to describe their professional accomplishments and personal characteristics, their difficulties and aspirations. The applications that I think are most disappointing are those that talk about only one dimension. All four or five essays will talk about an element of their job, or their personal life, or a particular aspect of their professional accomplishments. This inability or unwillingness to capture the variety of life contrasts greatly with the multi-thematic flavor we see in the applications of successful candidates.

We also have an essay on describing an ethical dilemma, how the candidate dealt with that dilemma, and whether or not they would have dealt with it differently in retrospect. I'm always surprised to see how many people don't understand what an ethical dilemma is. The answers we get for that question are often amusing.

11. What additional preparation or supplementary coursework might you recommend an applicant pursue to increase his or her chances for admission?

Linda   I think that for an individual who has either weak or limited quantitative exposure, it wouldn't hurt to take a calculus or statistics course. Some basic knowledge of common software applications is important. I also believe that macro- and microeconomics are courses that hit an individual quickly, and if you've had a prior exposure, that doesn't hurt. Most people who enter into MBA programs have had more than one exposure to economics before they take the econ class here at the MBA level. For someone who hasn't had any econ coursework, it might help them. It's not required, but it might be useful.

Although engineers frequently can handle most of the quantitative work, they may want to consider taking an international business course or another business-related class. Why? The more you've done to prepare yourself, whether it's reading or actual course work, full-time, transitional, or volunteer work experience, the more meaningful your essays are. When you start reading these applications, you look to see who has done his homework, who really wants this experience and has given it some thought. That's who you want in the program. Making the extra effort begins to build a bridge. It says to the reader, "I've got this interest, and guess how I'm pursuing it?" It's a commitment to continuous learning and personal development, and that's what we look for.

Marie As most business schools require pretty strong quantitative skills, for people who have been out of school for a while, I'd say go ahead and take an upper-level math class or statistics class—not because we want to see an A on your transcript, but because it says a lot about the student's initiative. We notice things like that. Also, for people for whom English is a second language, they should read and try to practice their English skills. For someone with a more quantitative background, if the applicant wanted to take a writing class, that would be great. I hope people aren't doing this just for the application process. When applicants take a course just to broaden their horizons, it says a lot about them and their commitment to learning.

Jon I think that anyone applying to a competitive MBA program is going to be applying to a program that wants balance. Instead of seeing candidates that have a narrowly defined group of accomplishments and capabilities, we appreciate when we see candidates with wide-ranging interests and a balance of skills. My recommendation is that candidates conduct a self-examination. Don't polish the gems that already shine. Try to be honest with yourself and ask, "What will committees see as my shortcomings?" and then address those issues. For an engineer, that might mean joining "Toastmasters." For the advertising executive, that might mean a course in calculus. More often than not, people will tend to overplay their strengths in the hopes that remarkable accomplishments in one area will compensate for weaknesses in another. Rather, it's balance that programs are looking for.

12. What one piece of advice would you give to a prospective candidate?

Linda Do your homework: Get to know the school. I know that sounds simple, but a lot of people don't invest the time needed to understand an MBA program—they shop too much. It is an effort that always pays off: If you do the homework, you get to know what the school environment is like, what the classes and the people are like. It's a big investment of both money and time, so it really is important for you to get to know as much as possible about the schools you think you want to attend and to know what it is that you want of these schools. The best people I've met are the ones who have made that commitment.

Try not to sound like everyone else. Don't take the advice, "This is how my application was, and this is how your application should be." If you do, you end up stuck in the pack, and there's no way you're going to get out of it. Really personalize your application. Try to give us who you are and what you want out of life.

Marie I canvassed my fellow staff members here, and we came up with pretty much the same answers. If we were talking to somebody who is definitely an applicant, we would say to him or her, spend quality time on your application—on your essays. If we were talking to someone at an MBA Forum who thought that he or she wanted to go back to business school but really wasn't sure, our piece of advice would be, sit down, read, talk to people, and figure out what the MBA is all about. And then, determine whether it is really something you need and want. Along with that, I'd encourage applicants to think about the MBA as a two-year experience. It's not just a credential. I hope people have an appreciation for the educational process that the MBA involves. That feeling is missing from a lot of applications. People just see it as "getting my ticket punched." Others think, "I want to change careers, so I need an MBA." That's fine and utilitarian, and, you're right, it will help you; but that's not what this place is all about. We're an academic institution. We care about the exchange of ideas, and we want to get a sense from an applicant that he understands that. Students are not in school again just to learn the current business trends and then leave—not here, anyway. There's a little bit more to an MBA than that. It's a new orientation, a new outlook, a new perspective, and I'm not always convinced that people understand that. The people who do and can communicate it well on paper really do stand out.

Jon Test drive the car before you buy. People are so eager to get into programs and are often diffident about their capabilities, that they're not aggressive enough about examining, challenging, and questioning the nature and quality of the programs to which they're applying. This is likely to be the last formal education of any kind you'll see. Thus, you should be as critical and judicious about selecting a program as the programs will be in selecting you.

13. If your program holds interviews, who do you interview? What is the purpose of the interview?

Linda   Our interviews are not required; we interview anyone who wants to talk with us. These interviews are an opportunity for the prospective applicants to get to know us better and to tell us about themselves, particularly if they feel parts of their "case" won't come across well on the application. Perhaps some issues are sensitive and need to be discussed in person. The interviews are also an opportunity for applicants to ask questions that they may have and, in some cases, to seek advice. This is particularly true for younger applicants. They can do that in a one-on-one. The interview is encouraged, but not mandatory.

We also do interviews of denied applicants so that they have a chance to learn why they've been denied. It keeps us honest. In addition, we interview waitlisted candidates, candidates about whom we need to learn more before we can make a decision either to admit or deny.

Jon   In the last four or five years, no one in the United States to whom we have extended an offer of admission was admitted without having interviewed. The only people we don't interview are about 40 percent of the international group. We just don't have the resources or the alumni to interview all of the international applicants.

In the last two years, all of our interviews have been conducted on campus; that's to force people to look at us as carefully as we look at them. We're trying to make an assessment of an applicant's interpersonal and communication skills, in part because success in a case-method program depends as much on communications skills as it does on analytical ability. We believe that this is also true in the working world, that an individual's long term success as a manager depends more on his people skills than on his analytical capabilities. Within two or three years, you're not going to be calculating net present value. You will be making decisions, gathering consensus, all those other things.

We conduct the interviews without having read the applications. If we read an application before meeting a candidate, we will inescapably form prejudgments about the candidates. If we interview someone who is lively and engaging, personable and dynamic, yet we know he had a 430 GMAT and a 2.5 GPA, he may suddenly appear facile, superficial, and slick. Or the dull-as-dishwater person with a 750 GMAT and a 3.9 then seems profound, deep, and subtle. So the less we know about a candidate prior to the interview, the more capable we are of making an independent judgment about his interpersonal and communication skills. Then, when we read the application, the interview, because it was independently derived from the other information, can bear more weight.

14. Who conducts your interviews? How long are they?

Linda   Admissions officers, alumni, and a select group of second-year students conduct our interviews. They are approximately 30 to 35 minutes in duration and give us additional information that we consider during the evaluation process. We get a valuable impression of you in these sessions, but the interview won't make you or break you. You've spent a lot of time putting your application together, and that should be more important than the 30 minutes you spend with us in an interview.

Jon   They tend to be an hour in length. My four colleagues and I do most of the interviews. Second-year students, some of whom are members of the admissions committee (we spend about four hours every fall training these people), also participate. In those situations outside the United States where we don't go or can't interview, we try to use our alums to do so.

15. Can students request interviews?

Linda   Yes.

Marie   No.

Jon   Yes; up until the first of March, all interviews are initiated by the candidates. We begin the interview process in September, so we give them several months to set up interviews at their discretion. After the first of March, if people have applied and have not scheduled interviews, and the admissions committee feels that an interview would be helpful for someone, then we will request an interview.

16. What turns you off most in an interview?

Linda   A couple of things: Having it as a "resume read" is one. I can read your resume myself. I'm really not excited by someone who has nothing more to tell me than what's on the resume. That turns me off, because they really are missing the point of the interview. Another thing that bothers me is when an individual comes to an interview without much knowledge of the program or is passive throughout the session. I like the person who takes the initiative in the interview, feels comfortable, and doesn't make it an assessment of himself. The interview is meant to be a dialogue; I don't shoot questions at you to see how you dodge. I'm really there to talk *with* you, not *to* you. I say that to each person who comes into my office. I want to get to know you better, to see how you fit here; and I want you to get to know us better, to see if we're the right school for you. That's the exchange we have going here. The kind of person who is engaging, who wants to raise questions that she has, discuss things about herself or observations she has made, is the type who will use the interview to her advantage. Someone who asks for the time and then comes in without really knowing how to use that half hour raises serious questions in our minds during the decision-making process.

Jon   People who come in with their own agendas and are inflexible. Therefore, they don't respond to the questions. They try to set the direction of the interview to meet a particular purpose. This reflects, to us, inflexibility, immaturity, and an inability to listen, all of which are essential to being a success in business.

17. If your institution does not conduct interviews of MBA-program applicants, why is that the case?

Marie   That's a good question. I don't think there is a shared philosophy on this quite yet within the admissions office. Interviews are something we've talked about and have toyed with; but right now, we haven't figured out a way to uniformly interview all of our candidates.

The various personalities you see reflected here are as different as the schools they represent. Despite the contrasts, however, among the three, it is also clear that certain themes have a consistent ring from person to person. Picking up on these themes will help you in thinking about some of the issues you may want to address in your positioning messages and, correspondingly, in your essays. The distinct character of each respondent, however, is also a good reminder of the fact that the schools, too, are quite different, that they all have unique identities, curriculums, and positionings within the business school "market." Part of your marketing challenge in the application process is to understand the spirit and style of each school and to ensure that your marketing messages take these differences into account.

Like those in Chapter 9, these interviews give you a taste of the flavor of the different programs. Conversations with alumni and current students, campus visits, and your other market research efforts will give you a further feeling for the nature of the different schools. All the research and planning in the world, however, is no substitute for the real thing. Take your best shot; we're sure you'll end up with some excellent options. What's more, the personal marketing skills you have developed during this process will be ones you can use throughout your life, whether you're applying for jobs or running for office. So head off to school and plunge right in. Business school can be one of the most engaging experiences in your life if you choose to make it so. We're confident you will.

Appendixes

The Top 25 Business Schools, *U.S. News & World Report*, 1995 Survey Results

	Average '94 GMAT	% Employed 3 months after graduation
1. Massachusetts Institute of Technology (Sloan)	650	98.0
2. University of Pennsylvania (Wharton)	650	99.0
3. Stanford University	680	96.0
4. Harvard University	635	95.0
5. Northwestern University (Kellogg)	638	95.0
6. Dartmouth College (Tuck)	660	92.0
7. University of Chicago	650	97.0
8. Duke University (Fuqua)	624	96.8
9. University of Virginia (Darden)	643	99.0
10. University of California at Berkeley (Haas)	647	95.0

(continued)

	Average '94 GMAT	% Employed 3 months after graduation
11. University of Michigan at Ann Arbor	630	95.0
12. Columbia University	640	97.0
13. University of California at Los Angeles (Anderson)	640	90.0
14. Carnegie Mellon University	640	97.0
15. Cornell University (Johnson)	630	94.0
16. Yale University	656	90.9
17. New York University (Stern)	627	93.0
18. University of North Carolina at Chapel Hill (Kenan/Flagler)	621	88.0
19. University of Texas at Austin	625	93.0
20. Purdue University (Krannert)	603	92.0
21. Indiana University at Bloomington	610	94.0
22. Georgetown University	618	93.0
23. Emory University (Goizueta)	625	90.0
24. University of Rochester (Simon)	604	94.0
25. Ohio State University (Fisher)	608	98.0

B

The Top 25 Business Schools: A Directory

Carnegie Mellon University
Graduate School of Industrial
 Administration
Schenley Park
5000 Forbes Avenue
Pittsburgh, PA 15213
412-268-2272
Fax: 412-268-6837
E-mail: GSIA-ADMISSIONS+@
 ANDREW.CMU.EDU

Columbia University Business
 School
Office of Admissions
105 Uris Hall
New York, NY 10027
212-854-1961
Fax: 212-662-6754

Cornell University
Johnson Graduate School of
 Management
Malett Hall
Ithaca, NY 14853
800-847-2082
Fax: 607-254-8886

Dartmouth College
The Amos Tuck School of
 Business Administration
100 Tuck Hall
Hanover, NH 03755-9030
603-646-3162
Fax: 603-646-1308

Duke University
The Fuqua School of Business
Box 90104
Durham, NC 27708-0104
919-660-7705
Fax: 919-681-8026

Emory University
The Roberta C. Goizueta Business
 School
1602 Mazell Drive
Atlanta, GA 30322-2710
404-727-6311
Fax: 404-727-4612

Georgetown University
Graduate School of Business
105 Old North Building
37th and O Street NW
Washington, DC 20057
202-687-4200
Fax: 202-687-7809

Harvard University
Graduate School of Business
 Administration
Soldiers Field
Boston, MA 02163
617-495-6127
Fax: 617-496-9272

Indiana University at
 Bloomington
Graduate School of Business
10th and Fee Lane, Room 254
Bloomington, IN 47405
812-855-8006
Fax: 812-855-9039

Massachusetts Institute of
 Technology
Sloan School of Management
50 Memorial Drive
Cambridge, MA 02139
617-253-3767
Fax: 617-253-6405
E-mail: MASTER'S@
 SLOAN.MIT.EDU

New York University
Leonard N. Stern School of
 Business
44 West Fourth Street, Suite 10-160
New York, NY 10012
212-998-0100
Fax: 212-995-4231

Northwestern University
J.L. Kellogg Graduate School of
 Management
Leverone Hall
2001 Sheridan Road
Evanston, IL 60208-2001
708-491-3308
Fax: 708-491-4960

Ohio State University
Fisher College of Business
Hagerty Hall
1775 College Road
Columbus, OH 43210
614-292-8511
Fax: 614-292-1651

Purdue University
Krannert School of Management
1310 Krannert Building
West Lafayette, IN 47907
317-494-4365
Fax: 317-494-9841

Stanford University
Graduate School of Business
350 Memorial Way
Stanford, CA 94305-5015
415-723-2766
Fax: 415-725-7831
E-mail: SINQUIRIES@
 GSB-PESO.STANFORD.EDU

University of California at
 Berkeley
Walter A. Haas School of Business
350 Barrows Hall
Berkeley, CA 94720
510-642-1405
Fax: 510-643-6659

University of California at Los
 Angeles
John E. Anderson Graduate
 School of Management
405 Hilgard Ave
Los Angeles, CA 90024
310-825-6944
Fax: 310-825-8582

The University of Chicago
Graduate School of Business
1101 East 58th Street
Chicago, IL 60637
312-702-7369
Fax: 312-702-9085

University of Michigan
School of Business Administration
Room 2260
Ann Arbor, MI 48109-1234
313-763-5796
Fax: 313-763-7804

University of North Carolina at
 Chapel Hill
Kenan-Flagler Business School
Campus Box No. 3490
Carroll Hall
Chapel Hill, NC 27599
919-962-3237
Fax: 919-962-0898

University of Pennsylvania
Wharton MBA Program
102 Vance Hall
3733 Spruce Street
Philadelphia, PA 19104-6361
215-898-3030, 3430, 6183
Fax: 215-898-0120

University of Rochester
William E. Simon Graduate School
 of Business Administration
Rochester, NY 14627
716-275-3533
Fax: 716-461-8382

University of Texas at Austin
Graduate School of Business
Austin, TX 78712
512-471-7612
Fax: 512-471-4243

University of Virginia
Darden Graduate School of
 Business Administration
PO Box 6550
Charlottesville, VA 22906
800-UVA-MBA1
Fax: 804-924-4859

Yale University
Yale School of Management
Box 1A
New Haven, CT 06520
203-432-5938
Fax: 203-432-6316

C

Information Checklist

After reading Chapter 2, Market Research, you may find this list useful as a method of keeping track of your research steps. The blanks at the bottom are for you to add your own personalized information

	Schools				
	A	B	C	D	E
General school information					
Application packet					
Application on diskette					
Financial aid information					
Interview schedule					
City visits/information sessions					
MBA forum					
Diversity brochures					
Non-MBA catalogs					

(continued)

	Schools				
	A	**B**	**C**	**D**	**E**
Personal interviews of alumni, friends, co-workers					
Professors, names in field of interest					
Student group contacts					

D

Tracking the Details

Here is a chart that we created to help us track the various pieces of the application. We originally developed this in a spreadsheet format and typed in completion dates and contact names as appropriate.

	Schools				
	A	B	C	D	E
Application requested					
Financial aid information requested					
Application received					
Financial aid information received					
Application deadline					
Transcript-request forms submitted to undergraduate institution					
Transcript received					
GMAT/TOEFL scores requested					
GMAT/TOEFL scores received					

(continued)

	Schools				
	A	B	C	D	E
Interview scheduled					
Campus visit scheduled					
Letters-of-recommendation forms submitted to recommenders					
Recommendation received					
Thank you to recommenders					
Administrative pages of the application completed					
Essays completed					
Financial aid form completed					

E

Diversity at the Top 25 Business Schools

Full-Time Program Information

School	% minority	% women	% of int'l students	Entering class size
Carnegie Mellon University	14	18	34	200
Columbia University	6	30	30	450
Cornell University (Johnson)	11	23	25	275
Dartmouth College (Tuck)	10	30	9.3	170
Duke University (Fuqua)	13	27	15	329
Emory University	18	37	18	126
Georgetown University	14	36	27	200
Harvard University	18	29	26	800
Indiana University at Bloomington	15	30	14	232
MIT (Sloan)	8	25	30	265

(continued)

School	% minority	% women	% of int'l students	Entering class size
New York University (Stern)	16	29	28	463
Northwestern University (Kellogg)	18	30	24	491
Ohio State University (Fisher)	11	34	25	138
Purdue University	15	36	26	156
Stanford University	18	26	23	353
University of California at Berkeley (Haas)	19	26	29	223
University of California at Los Angeles (Anderson)	19	27	19	309
University of Chicago	8	25	20	550
University of Michigan	22	13	30	432
University of N. Carolina at Chapel Hill (Kenan-Flagler)	14	33	12	195
University of Pennsylvania (Wharton)	15	26	33	786
University of Rochester (Simon)	15	22	42	200

(continued)

School	% minority	% women	% of Int'l students	Entering class size
University of Texas at Austin	22	33	18	460
University of Virginia (Darden)	17	29	12	256
Yale University	12	33	34	220

F

Assessment of MBA Programs

We found it useful to create a chart such as this and rank programs on a scale of 1 to 10 to help us prioritize our choices of schools. Everyone will weight these factors differently, so you should apply your own weighting to arrive at a total score. Again, this list is by no means exhaustive.

	Schools				
	A	B	C	D	E
General reputation					
Academic vigor					
Academic match with personal interests					
Ability to opt out of classes					
Size of classes					
Strength of professors					
Post-MBA placement					
Average salary					
Reputation in the region/country of your interest					

(continued)

	Schools				
	A	B	C	D	E
Peer group					
Teamwork					
Social environment					
Location/weather					
Financial cost					
Financial assistance					
Alumni network					
Size of alumni pool					
National vs. international					
Family issues					

Index

About the Authors

After receiving their MBAs from the Harvard Business School in 1994, Phil and Carol Carpenter fled the brutal Boston winters for a more civilized existence in Menlo Park, California. Phil is now a high-tech marketing consultant for Regis McKenna, Inc., and Carol is a product marketing manager for the Power Macintosh at Apple Computer.

While at Harvard, both writers served as admissions counselors for the Harvard Business School Admissions Office, leading weekly information sessions for prospective applicants. In 1992, they applied and were accepted to 11 MBA programs: Harvard, Wharton, Kellogg, the MIT Sloan School of Management, UCLA, the University of Chicago, Duke, the University of Virginia, Dartmouth's Tuck School of Business Administration, the University of North Carolina, and the University of Michigan.